© Copyright   GEORGE STEINHAUER - MICHALIS TOUBIS
                     PUBLICATIONS S.A.
                     Nisiza Karela, Koropi, Attiki.
                     Telephone: +30 210 6029974, Fax: +30 210 6646856
                     Web Site: http://www.toubis.gr

ISBN: 960-540-500-8

GEORGE STEINHAUER

Ephor of Antiquities

THE MONUMENTS AND ARCHAEOLOGICAL MUSEUM OF PIRAEUS

Stele with palmette from Eëtioneia
(4th c. BC)

CONTENTS

HISTORY AND ARCHAEOLOGICAL SITES

BRIEF HISTORICAL INTRODUCTION 9

A STROLL IN SEARCH OF THE ANCIENT TOWN
BENEATH THE MODERN 14
The walls and gates of ancient Piraeus 14
The Shipyard and the Emporion 18
Sacred and Private Space 22

THE ARCHAEOLOGICAL MUSEUM
.... 26

RECEPTION AND INFORMATION AREA 29

FIRST FLOOR

ROOM 1 (vestibule)
The shipyard and the agora. Sanctuaries of Attica 30

ROOM 2
Pottery and small finds from the Mycenaean
to the Hellenistic period (1500-300 BC) 35
Everyday life and art in the Classical period 40

ROOM 3
Archaic sculpture –
the bronze Apollo of Piraeus 46

ROOM 4
Bronze statues of the 4th c. BC 49

ROOM 5
The sanctuary of the Mother of the Gods (Cybele)
at Moschato. Reconstruction of an ancient sanctuary...........57

ROOM 6
Grave stelai 420-350 BC
The repertoire of Classical grave reliefs
in the rooms of the Piraeus Museum.................................63

GROUND FLOOR
ROOMS 7 and 8
Grave stelai and funerary monuments 350 - 317 BC...................75

ROOM 9
Sculptures of the Hellenistic period.................................86

ROOM 10
Art of the Roman period.................................88

NOTES - BIBLIOGRAPHY.................................94

COLOUR PLATES OF EXHIBITS ....97 - 126

The Eëtioneia Gate at the beginning of the 20th century (photograph of the German Archaeological Institute)

HISTORY AND ARCHAEOLOGICAL SITES

BRIEF HISTORICAL INTRODUCTION

The three harbours of the barren peninsula of Piraeus and its proximity to Athens, the political centre of Attica, were decisive factors both in the initial settlement of humans here and in the characteristic mobility of the population of Piraeus since that time and the historical vicissitudes of the town. The foundation and the flowering of Piraeus in both ancient and modern times, have been inextricably linked with the fortunes of Athens.

Little is known of the earliest history of Piraeus. In ancient times, a memory was retained (Harpokration, Strabo) of a period when it was still an island in an enormous bay of Phaleron, which stretched from cape Kolias, at Aï Yorgis in Palio Faliro, to the rock of Eëtioneia at Drapetsona. A relic of this bay survived in Classical times in the form of the marshy plain of Halipedon, which encircled Piraeus from Neo Faliro to Kaminia, isolating the Piraeus peninsula from the rest of Attica.

This accounts for the choice of Palio Faliro, near Aï Yorgis, for the location of the first harbour of Athens, and also for the confinement of habitation to the area of Munychia, around the strategic hill of Profitis Ilias and the secure harbour of Tourkolimano, where the ancient sanctuary of Artemis (finds dating from as early as the Middle Bronze Age) is to be found.

The deme of Piraeus, created by Kleisthenes after 510 BC, was part of a union of four demes *(tetrakomia)* that included the neighbouring demes of Thymiatadai (modern Keratsini), Xypete (Kaminia-Rendis-Moschato) and Phaleron. The religious centre of this union was a sanctuary of Herakles at Kaminia.

Piraeus, however, was preeminently the creation of Themistokles. It was Themistokles who not only recognised the importance of its geographical location and its three harbours to the future of Athens, but who also proceeded, even before the Persian Wars, to provide it with the fortifications that are still the most impressive remains of the ancient city.

Construction of the town began immediately after the departure of the Persians, more specifically about 470-460 BC according to the earliest finds, to designs by the father of town-planning, Hippodamos of Miletos. The shipyard was laid out and linked with Athens by way of the Long Walls, a project begun by Kimon in 460 BC and completed by Perikles ten years later through the construction of the middle wall. These developments formed the basis of an Athens that was impregnable by land: a city that was now mistress of a naval empire, and of which Piraeus was the military, commercial-financial, and to some extent the political centre for a period of over a hundred years – from 470 BC to about 350 BC – with a few interruptions.

The strategic significance of the new town was the reason behind the triumphant demolition of its fortifications and the Long Walls by the Spartans after the end of the Peloponnesian War in 404 BC, and also for their rapid reconstruction by Konon, using Persian money, after the victorious battle of Knidos in 394 BC. For the 4th century flowering of trade and the general economic life of Piraeus, we possess a wealth of information from the orators, mainly Demosthenes, and from the monuments.

The will and determination of Athens to maintain her naval

hegemony in the Aegean, which did not falter, even after the defeat at Chaironeia in 338 BC, is attested by the continuous increase in the size of the fleet and the construction of 372 shipsheds, which at this time spread in an asphyxiating arc around the military harbours of Zea and Munychia, as well as part of the commercial harbour and the Arsenal of Philo. With tragic irony, the Arsenal was completed a few years before the destruction of the Athenian fleet at the battle of Amorgos in 322 BC. For the larger part of the third century, Piraeus and particularly the fort of Munychia was a bastion of the Macedonian domination of Attica, and at the same time a link in the chain of Macedonian fortresses controlling Greece. After liberation, in 229 BC, Athens was restricted to the role of cultural capital of the Hellenistic and then the Roman world, and the importance of Piraeus was diminished. The famous dockyard was thereafter a huge empty shell (the *karyon kenon* of the comic writers).

The beginning of the Roman period was marked by the long siege and destruction of Piraeus (86 BC) that was the consequence of Athens' collaboration with Mithridates. The symbols of Athens' naval strength, the Shipsheds and Arsenal, were put to the torch. Piraeus was abandoned and occupation confined, according to Strabo, to the area around the harbour and the temple of Zeus Soter. The town never exceeded these boundaries, despite efforts to restore it by Pompey, Augustus, and Hadrian, and in the Early Byzantine period. In Post-Byzantine times, Piraeus was completely abandoned, apart from the monastery of Ayios Spyridon, the customs-house (Dogana) and a single residence, which survived down to the Greek War of Independence. Even its name was forgotten. At this period it was called Porto Leone or Porto Draco, after a gigantic statue of a lion that stood at the head of the harbour. Morosini, to whom is owed the oldest map of the region (with drawings of the fortifications of Munychia), took this monument with him when he left, and it now adorns the entrance to the dockyard in Venice.

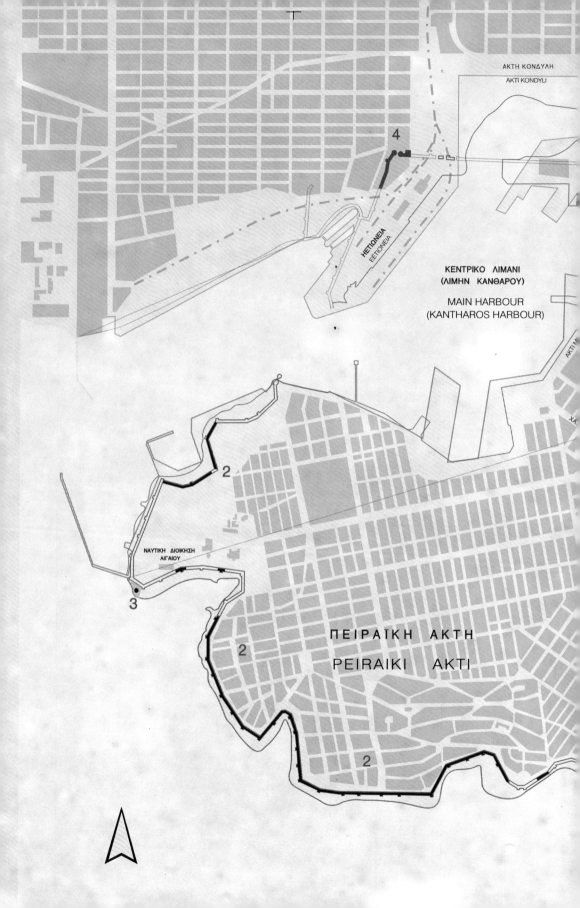

ΑΚΤΗ ΚΟΝΔΥΛΗ
AKTI KONDYLI

4

ΗΕΤΙΩΝΕΙΑ
ΕΕΤΙΟΝΕΙΑ

ΚΕΝΤΡΙΚΟ ΛΙΜΑΝΙ
(ΛΙΜΗΝ ΚΑΝΘΑΡΟΥ)

MAIN HARBOUR
(KANTHAROS HARBOUR)

2

ΝΑΥΤΙΚΗ ΔΙΟΙΚΗΣΗ
ΑΙΓΑΙΟΥ

3

2

ΠΕΙΡΑΪΚΗ ΑΚΤΗ

PEIRAIKI ΑΚΤΙ

2

2

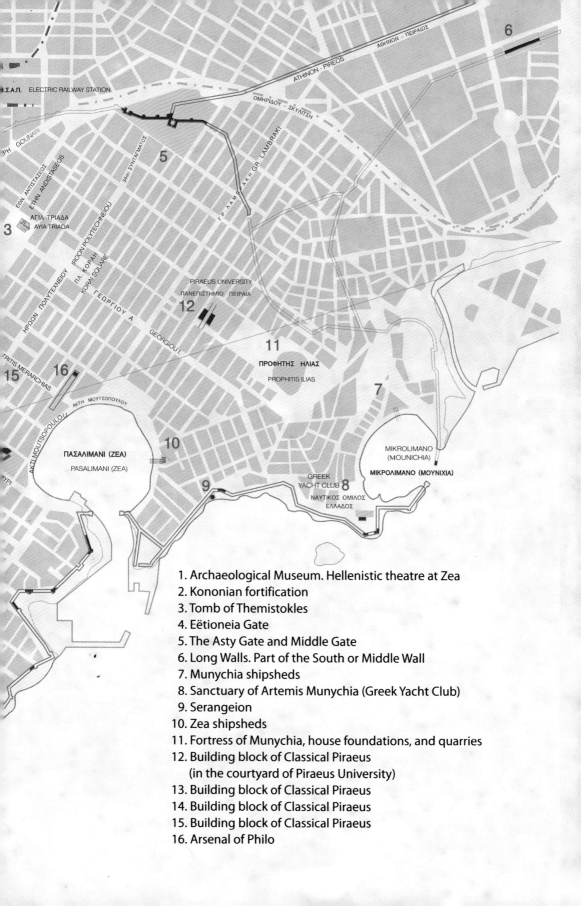

ΗΣΑΠ ELECTRIC RAILWAY STATION

ΑΘΗΝΩΝ - ΠΕΙΡΑΙΩΣ
ATHINON - PIREOS

ΟΜΗΡΙΔΟΥ - ΣΚΥΛΙΤΣΗ

6

PH. GOUNARI

3

ΕΘΝ. ΑΝΤΙΣΤΑΣΕΩΣ
ETHN. ANDISTASEOS

ΑΓΙΑ·ΤΡΙΑΔΑ
AYIA TRIADA

ΗΡΩΩΝ ΠΟΛΥΤΕΧΝΕΙΟΥ
IROON POLYTECHNEIOU

ΠΛ. ΚΟΡΑΗ
KORAI SQUARE

ΓΕΩΡΓΙΟΥ Α
GEORGIOU I.

34ο ΣΥΝΤΑΓΜΑΤΟΣ

ΓΡ. ΛΑΜΠΡΑΚΗ GR. LAMBRAKI

5

PIRAEUS UNIVERSITY
ΠΑΝΕΠΙΣΤΗΜΙΟ ΠΕΙΡΑΙΑ

12

11

ΠΡΟΦΗΤΗΣ ΗΛΙΑΣ
PROPHITIS ILIAS

7

TRITIS MERARCHIAS

15

16

ΑΚΤΗ ΜΟΥΤΣΟΠΟΥΛΟΥ
AKTI MOUTSOPOULOU

10

ΠΑΣΑΛΙΜΑΝΙ (ΖΕΑ)
PASALIMANI (ZEA)

ΜΙΚΡΟΛΙΜΑΝΟ
(MOUNICHIA)

ΜΙΚΡΟΛΙΜΑΝΟ (ΜΟΥΝΙΧΙΑ)

9

GREEK
YACHT CLUB 8
ΝΑΥΤΙΚΟΣ ΟΜΙΛΟΣ
ΕΛΛΑΔΟΣ

1. Archaeological Museum. Hellenistic theatre at Zea
2. Kononian fortification
3. Tomb of Themistokles
4. Eëtioneia Gate
5. The Asty Gate and Middle Gate
6. Long Walls. Part of the South or Middle Wall
7. Munychia shipsheds
8. Sanctuary of Artemis Munychia (Greek Yacht Club)
9. Serangeion
10. Zea shipsheds
11. Fortress of Munychia, house foundations, and quarries
12. Building block of Classical Piraeus
    (in the courtyard of Piraeus University)
13. Building block of Classical Piraeus
14. Building block of Classical Piraeus
15. Building block of Classical Piraeus
16. Arsenal of Philo

A STROLL IN SEARCH OF THE ANCIENT TOWN BENEATH THE MODERN

The walls and gates of ancient Piraeus

The best-preserved ancient remains are the ruins of the fortifications, which still set the tone of the modern town to those approaching from the sea or from Athens. According to Thucydides (II 13.1), the total length of the original (Themistoklean) fortifications of Piraeus was 60 stades (the stade is reckoned to have been 177.60 m.). Measurements by von Alten, who made measured drawings in 1879 *(Karten von Attika)*, suggest that in its final (Kononian) form, the enceinte was 13 km. long, or about 80 stades.

The coastal section of the fortification walls along the Peiraiki Akti is today preserved for a length of 2.5 km. in the form in which it was built by Konon in 394 BC – that is, by the *emplektos* technique, consisting of two facing walls filled with rubble and earth, with a total width of 3.10 m. The wall is preserved up to a height of as many as 8 courses and it is possible that it was constructed of stone for its full height. Twenty-two (of the originally fifty-five) towers are preserved, separated by distances ranging from 45 to 100 m., depending on the nature of the coast. The facade of the towers is 6.50 m. wide, they project 5.50 from the curtain walls, and there is usually a small gate 1.20-1.50 m. wide beside them. Behind each of the towers can be found the foundations, 9 m. long and 1.30 m. wide, of its stone staircase. What is perhaps the only section of the Themistoklean wall (solidly built) stands at the entrance to the harbour of Zea, beneath the modern bridge. In the ancient harbours, the fortification wall did not continue along the coast, but stopped at the entrance, where it ended in two towers that could be connected by a chain. One such tower is still preserved at the entrance to the Zea harbour, on the Kastella side, and there is another at the entrance to Tourkolimano

(Munychia). The corresponding moles *(cheilai)* and towers that closed off the main harbour were destroyed after 1830. Near the entrance to the outer mole, in the area of the offices of the Naval Administration of the Aegean, now out of bounds to the public, there is a grave enclosure outside the fortification walls with a (restored) column, which has been identified with the tomb of Themistokles ever since ancient times.

The land (north) section of the fortifications can be seen only in the area of the gates, at the precise point where, in 493 BC, before the building of the town had even begun, Themistokles began work on the enceinte by erecting a statue of Hermes by the Gate. This point is the most vulnerable in the Piraeus fortifications, and the wall was accordingly made thicker (5 m.) and given a solid structure. It is described admiringly by Thucydides (I 93): *In breadth the wall was built according to his specifications, just as one can see it today around Piraeus. There was room for two wagons to pass each other with their stones for the building, and the space in between the outer surfaces was not filled in with rubble or clay; instead large blocks of stone were cut and fitted together, with clamps of iron and lead on the outside. The height of the finished wall was about half what he planned. With these great and thick walls he intended to repulse all enemy attacks, and he considered that they could be perfectly well defended by a few troops of inferior quality, so that the rest would be able to serve in the navy* (translation: Rex Warner, Penguin edition). Appian also provides information on the height and construction of the wall in describing the brave resistance of Piraeus to the siege by Sulla in 86 BC (Mithridates 30): *The walls were 40 cubits (18.50 m.) high and were made of large dressed stones.*

The main gates of Piraeus are at the entrance to the modern town, on the main axis of Triakostou Tetartou Syntagmatos – Iroön Polytechneiou Streets, the only natural route that secures rapid access to the harbour for anyone travelling from Athens. The two gates of Piraeus are not contemporary with each other.

The Asty Gate and the carriage road *(hamaxitos)* **to Athens.** The earliest gate, the *Town or Asty Gate,* is the westernmost gate, on the right as one enters the town; it is now enclosed by Pylis, Omiridou, Skylitsi and Kolokotroni Streets. In the first, Themistoklean, building phase, the towers were circular (oval, to be more precise) and were replaced by rectangular towers during the reconstruction of the walls by Konon in 394 BC. The distance separating the towers is 15 m. and the one at the west projects by 8 m. This creates a first, exterior space in which to engage the enemy, whose right side would be exposed (the shield covered only the left), before he was trapped and assaulted on all sides in the inner courtyard. The main carriage road, or *hamaxitos*, to Athens passed through the Asty Gate, the opening of which was 6.75 m. wide.

The Long Walls and the Middle Gate. About thirty years after the beginning of the erection of the Themistoklean fortifications at Piraeus, work began on the construction of the Long Walls that were to link Athens with its harbour. The northern wall, now beneath Pireos Street, and the Phaleric wall, now lost (though it seems to have ended at Aï Yorgis at Palio Faliro) were built by Kimon in 460 BC. The Attic basin remained unprotected from the sea. Perikles later built the middle or southern wall, which can still be seen at many parts of Neo Faliro (e.g. at the intersection of Soultani and Emmanouilidou Streets and in the complex of worker's apartment blocks on Kanellopoulou Street, behind the ELAIS factory) and Moschato (along the south side of the railway track). These walls created a secure corridor, 180 m. wide, between the two cities, forming an impregnable island that served as a safe refuge for the population of Attica during the Peloponnesian War. When the middle wall was constructed, it became necessary to create a second, middle gate near the Asty Gate, for traffic using the corridor of the Long Walls. This second gate, which has been entirely uncovered, is very imposing. Access to it is from Zanni Street. It is very similar to the Dipylon Gate in Athens, though it is significantly smaller: the main

Tower in the Kononian Wall on the Peraiki Akti.

The Gate through the Long Walls.

courtyard is 18 m. long and 16.5 m. wide. At the entrance opening (4 m. wide) traces of the door mechanism can be detected, and there are wheelmarks in the road that passed through the gate.

The Eëtioneia Gate. On the north side of the Kantharos harbour, on the Kastraki hill at Drapetsona, the imposing gate of the fortress of Eëtioneia rises menacingly, now disencumbered of the rubble that used to cover it and of the buildings of the Customs House that once concealed it. This area was included in the Themistoklean wall from the very beginning. The 'castle', however – that is, the gate and the cross-wall – were built in 411 by the oligarchs of Athens, with the aim of controlling the harbour and possibly surrendering it to the Spartans. The gate is of simple type, with no inner courtyard, and consists of an entrance 3.70 m. wide which, at a later date, probably in the Hellenistic period, was flanked by two circular towers about 10 m. in diameter and with a preserved height today of at least 2 m. Two sections of wall start from this gate. The first, which runs west towards the harbour, is solidly built and follows the course of the original fortification. The second, which runs towards the outer harbour is built mainly in the *emplektos* technique. The wall is only 2.70-3.50 m. thick, but is protected by a deep moat dug into the rock, leaving only a narrow passage in front of the gate.

The Shipyard and the Emporion

If Piraeus owes its existence to Themistokles, its urban design is the only certainly attested work by the father of town-planning (Aristotle, Politics 1267e: *Hippodamos son of Euryphontos of Miletos, who discovered the division of cities and laid out the Piraeus*). The principle of Hippodamos's work was the rational organisation of the urban space, based on its division into public, private and sacred areas and the separation of its basic functions: its military role, its function as the shipyard of Athens, and its commercial function as the leading commercial harbour in the Mediterranean.

Of the ancient shipyard, which formed the foundation of the strength of the Athenian empire and indirectly of the flowering of the arts in Athens, all that now survives and is open to the public are parts of three shipsheds in the Zea harbour, and the entrance to the famous Arsenal of Philo. Both sites are situated a short distance from the Museum.

The **shipsheds** are simple sheds that share a roof *(homotegeis)* and a continuous back wall. They are divided by colonnades into parallel bays 41 m. long and 6.50 m. wide. Between the colonnades was a crepis, either dug into the rock or stone-built, which has a wooden floor and a channel for the keel of the ships. This structure was used for pulling up the triremes. In the 4th c. BC there were 372 shipsheds in Piraeus: 196 at Zea, 82 at Munychia, and 94 in the main Kantharos harbour. The only preserved part of the shipsheds known until recently is in a semi-basement area of the apartment block at Sirangeiou Street 1. It forms part of a larger complex that extended to the surrounding streets and the garden of the neighbouring stone neogothic house on Akti Moutsopoulou. In 1997, a large section of the shipsheds of Munychia was discovered on the coast at Tourkolimano. To prevent sabotage, the shipyard was protected by an enclosure wall, part of which has been discovered behind the shipsheds of both Zea and Munychia. This section of wall can now be seen in the alley behind the refugee houses in Tourkolimano.

The Arsenal *(Skeuotheke)* of Philo was one of the finest buildings in the port of Piraeus. It was a huge (138 m. long) storehouse for hanging equipment (sails, ropes, cables, etc.), and was named after its architect Philo. Work began on it in 347/6 and was not completed until 323/2 BC. It was destroyed by Sulla in 86 BC. An inscription found in 1882 near Kanari Square provided a detailed description *(syngraphe)* of the building, which consisted of a central aisle and two rows of storerooms with lofts in the side aisles. The *skeuotheke* itself, which was believed to have been completely destroyed, was found by chance in 1988-1989. The north entrance, with its double door and the beginnings of the two rows of pillars forming the central aisle, can be visited in the open grounds, now appropriately laid out, of an office building at Ypsilandou Street 170. Another part of the building has been excavated and is now concealed beneath the surface of Defteras Merarchias Street.

The *Emporion* (the commercial sector of Kantharos harbour). There are far fewer physical remains of the commercial harbour of ancient Piraeus. The original reason for this was a rise in the level of the sea, which had covered the ancient harbour installations already by the end of antiquity. Even the Late Roman ruins that were still preserved along the entire coast at the beginning of the 19th century rapidly vanished beneath the foundations of the quay, the moles and the streets of the port of the new capital. The precise location, extent and form of this part of Piraeus is known from the boundary markers *(horoi)*, found in the 19th century in their original positions. The commercial sector was divided off from the rest of the city by a street. At one point of this, at the intersection of the modern Kolokotroni and Sachtouri Streets, the boundary marker of the Emporion and street was found still standing in its original position. On the side near the sea, the boundaries of the commercial anchorage were again defined by two stelai bearing the inscription *'boundary of the bay of the ferries...'*. The Emporion therefore occupied the east coastal zone (an area of about 1.5 km.[2]) of the main harbour, stretching from the modern Atki Miaouli to about Notara Street, and from Karaïskaki Square in the north to the Customs House in the south. The character of this area was defined by five large stoas built around the harbour, and by the large mole *(Diazevgma)* that could still be seen in the 19th century in the middle of the area of the Emporion.

Traces of these stoas have been revealed by excavation. In the middle of the Emporion, opposite the *Diazevgma*, was the *Deigma*, where merchants displayed samples of imported goods. The *Large Stoa* stood at the north end of the harbour, next to the fortification wall. According to the inscription IG II[2] 1035, ship repair yards *(psyktrai)*

The entrance to the Arsenal of Philo.

extended outside the area of the large harbour enclosed by the shipsheds, the temple of Aphrodite and the stoas, as far as the chains that sealed off the entrance to the harbour.

Sacred and private space

Very few of the known monuments of the ancient city have survived. The agoras, the theatre of Dionysos, the sanctuary of Zeus Soter, the Asklepieion and the sanctuaries of the foreign gods, Cybele and Bendis, have probably been lost forever. The large theatre of Dionysos in Piraeus was located on the north slope of the Munychia hill, just below the visible section of the Macedonian fort, and part of the Asklepieion has been excavated on the west side of the same hill, above the Zea harbour (Pasalimani). This excavation yielded a relief of the healing of a woman, now on display in the Museum. The colossal cult statue of Asklepios from Munychia and other important sculptures have been taken to the National Archaeological Museum in Athens. On top of the hill, now laid out as a park, can be seen ancient quarries and the ruins of buildings, one of which is probably a small sanctuary of Artemis. Part of the sanctuary of Artemis Munychia (though not the temple itself) has been found and can still be seen in the foundations of the Yacht Club of Greece, on the strongly defended hill that controlled the entrance to the harbour of Munychia (now Tourkolimano). Antiquities found during excavations conducted by the Ephorate are preserved in basements or in suitably laid out archaeological sites. They still offer modern visitors to Piraeus a dense network of reference points for the history of the ancient city. Those who wish may stroll in an archaeological park, visiting houses, cisterns, quarries, workshops, sanctuaries and entire building blocks, dating from the 5th c. BC down to Roman times, which were part of the urban tissue of the city that was Hippodamos's first creation. The organisation of the space, the clear separation of functions, the equal distribution of plots, and the uniformity of the residences make Hippodamos's Piraeus a living lesson in rational design, human scale and democracy – *isonomia* as it was called by the ancient Greeks. The most interesting **survival of the ancient city,** with its wide streets, spacious houses with an *oikos* (family living-room) and an *andron* (banquet room), richly decorated with mosaics at the back of the courtyard is still preserved in a temporary **fill in the courtyard of the Piraeus University.** (A smaller surviving section can be visited in the basement of the **church of Ayia Triada.**) A number of monuments can also be seen in the **archaeological park in Iroön Polytechneiou Street,** and others have recently been excavated in the **Ralleios plot in Terpsithea.** In all three cases, the ruins of the Classical town are partly covered by later, much larger houses with a central peristyle courtyard or atrium and dating in the first case to the Hellenistic period and in the other two to Roman times.

Two other notable monuments survive from the 4th c. BC and the Hellenistic period. **A cave-installation belonging to a sanctuary with a bathhouse,** is dated to the 4th c. BC on the strength of its mosaics (with a chariot and depiction of Scylla), now lost. It is probably to be identified with the Serangeion, which was built on the rocks of Kastella, overlooking the sea. **The Hellenistic (2nd c. BC) theatre at Zea harbour,** in the garden of the archaeological museum, is of historical and typological interest, in that it is a smaller-scale copy of the theatre of Dionysos built by Lykourgos in Athens. All that survives of it is the stage-building and paraskenia, and the orchestra and front row of seats; all the facing of the cavea is missing.

The finds confirm Strabo's statement that by the Roman period Piraeus was confined to the area around the harbour. The buildings identified from time to time in this region, which is bounded on the south by Praxitelous Street, include large storage buildings, bathhouses and houses of the imperial period. The ruins of a Roman temple in the basement of an office building at Philonos Street 4 will soon be open to the public.

Further information on the history and topography of ancient Piraeus can be found in the following books: E. Curtius – J.A. Kaupert, *Karten von Attika, Heft 1,* Berlin 1881. W. Judeich, *Topographie von Athen,* 2nd ed. Munich 1931. Ch. Panagos, *Ο Πειραιεύς, Οικονομική και Ιστορική Έρευνα από των Αρχαιοτάτων Χρόνων,* Athens 1969, 2nd ed. with recent evidence for the topography of Piraeus added by G. Steinhauer, Athens 1995. J. Travlos, *Εγκυκλοπαίδεια Δομή,* 1972, entry on Piraeus. R. Garland, *The Piraeus from the Fifth to the First Century B.C.,* New York, 1987. J. Travlos, *Bildlexikon zur Topographie des antiken Attika,* 1988. K.-V. v Eickstedt, *Beiträge zur Topographie des antiken Piraeus,* Athens 1991. W. Hoepfner – E. Schandner, *Haus und Stadt im klassischen Griechenland,* Neubearbeitung, Munich 1994, pp. 22-50. G. Steinhauer, *Piraeus, Centre of Shipping and Culture,* Athens 2000.

Boundary marker of the agora.

Part of the ancient settlement, in the courtyard of Piraeus University.

THE ARCHAEOLOGICAL MUSEUM

The museum is in a sense the mirror of the life and functioning of the ancient city of Piraeus. The nature of the exhibits and the chronological period covered by the collection provide a representative picture of the distinctive character of the ancient city, the composition of its population, and its history, which was closely interlinked with the political and economic prosperity of Athens. In contrast with the *asty*,

The Archaeological Museum of Piraeus.

the city of Athens, where the official cults were concentrated and where Perikles' ambitious programme of sanctuary-building created works of unsurpassed size and luxury, the image of the harbour was defined by its fortifications, shipyard installations, the stoas in the commercial harbour, and Hippodamos's ground-breaking town plan. It is not surprising, therefore, that the display is dominated by finds of the 5th and 4th c. BC, most of them, such as the funerary monuments, associated with private life. The finds from the demes of Attica, which are also represented in the exhibition, have reference to the same sphere of life.

The first Archaeological Museum of Piraeus was built in 1935 on the north side of the Hellenistic theatre in the Zea harbour. It housed a collection that had gradually been assembled from donations, objects handed in by the public, chance finds, and items yielded by archaeological excavations. The original building was extended by the construction of the new museum, the foundations of which were laid in 1966. It is the main museum of the II Ephorate of Prehistoric and Classical Antiquities, in which archaeological finds mainly from the area of Piraeus, Salamis, and the coast as far as Varkiza, are assembled, conserved and housed. The museum has been considerably enriched by donations from large private collections, such as the Meletopoulos-Nomidis Collection and recently the Yeroulanos Collection. The foundations for the exhibition were laid by Thymios Mastrokostas, Olga Alexandri and Yorgos Despinis. The display was later extended by Vasilios Petrakos, with the transfer to the museum of the bronze statues kept in the National Archaeological Museum, the first, partial, restoration of the Kallithea Monument (1982), and the re-exhibition of the sanctuary of Cybele (1985). The museum has recently (1998) benefited greatly from Stelios Triandis's restoration of the Kallithea Monument and the exhibiting of the pottery collection and small finds.

The redesigning of the exhibition was supported financially by the President of the Association of the Friends of the Museum, Yannis Polychronopoulos, the Psychas Foundation, and Michalis Toubis. The study for the lighting of the exhibits is owed to Kimon Choursoglou.

The Hellenistic theatre at Zea, in the Museum garden.

RECEPTION AND INFORMATION AREA

The map displayed at the entrance, opposite the ticket office, provides information about the archaeological sites mentioned above, a tour of which form a desirable follow-up to a visit to the museum.

The path to be followed in the museum rooms is indicated on the diagram opposite the entrance. The visit begins in the vestibule on the first floor, which can be reached by elevator, and continues on the ground floor. The rooms are numbered according to the subject groups and chronological sequence of the exhibits. It ends with a visit to the museum garden, in which is the little Hellenistic theatre of Zea.

UPPER FLOOR

GROUND FLOOR

1. The agora and the dockyard.
   Sanctuaries of Attica
2. Pottery and small finds 1500-300 BC.
   Everyday life and art in the Classical period.
3. Archaic sculpture
   The Bronze Apollo of Piraeus
4. Bronze statues of the 4th c. BC.
5. The sanctuary of Cybele at Moschato.
   Reconstruction of a Classical sanctuary

6. Grave stelai 420-350 BC
7. Grave stelai and monuments 350-317 BC.
   The lion of Moschato
8. Grave stelai and monuments 350-317 BC.
   The funerary monument of Kallithea
9. Sculptures of the Hellenistic period
10. Art of the Roman period

FIRST FLOOR

ROOM 1 (VESTIBULE)

The shipyard and the agora. Sanctuaries of Attica

The vestibule on the first floor serves as a historical and thematic introduction to the ancient city as a commercial centre and a military shipyard. In front of the glass partition, is **the bronze ram from a trireme,** in the form of a trident **(pl. 1)** 0.80 m. long, which probably dates from the 4th c. BC. It was recently presented to the museum by Mr. Vasilios Kallios. This is a unique find, since all the other known rams come either from much smaller vessels (ship's beak in the Fitzwilliam Museum, Cambridge, ram in the Naval Museum, Bremerhaven, miniature ram in the Kanellopoulos Museum, Athens), or from much larger ones (Athlit ram in the Haifa Museum), and all of them are from much later ships. The large crack in the middle of the ram was probably caused by a head-on, collision that proved fatal to it.[1]* In the same showcase is a **marble eye from a trireme,** one of the best preserved of the eyes of various sizes found in Piraeus.[2] These were not dedications but objects with a practical use, as is indicated by the recent discovery of fragments of them in the foundations of the Arsenal of Philo. The colour of the iris can be made out. It has been attached to the back of the case in the same way as it was presumably fastened to the prow of the ship. To the right of this case is one of the numerous **stone pyramidal anchors** of various sizes kept in the museum; the rest are on display in the garden. Most of them come from the shipyard at Zea. They are of a

30

* The numbers refer to the notes at the end of the book.

The metrological relief from Salamis.

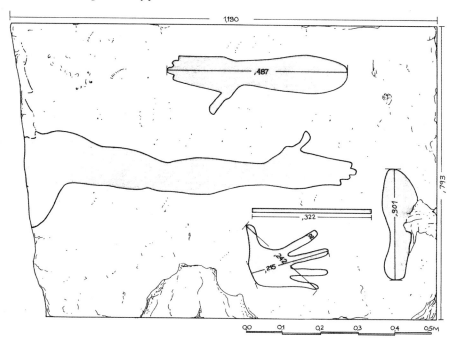

very ancient type widely found in the Mediterranean, though it is still a matter of debate whether they were anchors carried on board the ship, or more probably – according to a convincing theory – capstans, placed in a row, to which the triremes were tied before being pulled up into the shipsheds.[3]

The wall opposite is devoted to the commercial life of the harbour. The middle of it is occupied by **the metrological relief no. 5352 (pl. 2)** which was detached from a chapel on the island of Salamis. Metric units are represented in intaglio: half an *orgyia* (the length of the outstretched arms), the *pechys* (forearm) (0.487 m.), the *spithame* (span between the thumb and little finger) (0.242 m.) and the *pous* (foot). Two different metric systems are found together in the relief. The first is based on a standard measure of 0.322 m. – that is, the length

31

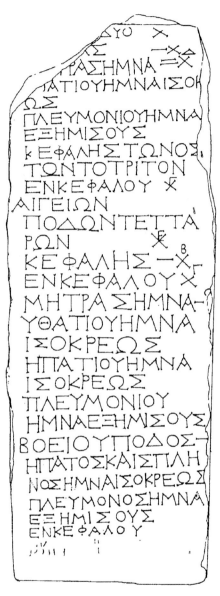

ΣΥΟ Χ
ΑΣ ΗΜΝΑ ＝Χ
ΑΤΙΟΥΗΜΝΑ ΙΣΟH
ΩΣ
ΠΛΕΥΜΟΝΙΟΥΗΜΝΑ
ΕΞΗΜΙΣΟΥΣ
ΚΕΦΑΛΗΣ ΤΩΝΟΣ
ΤΩΝΤΟΤΡΙΤΟΝ
ΕΝΚΕΦΑΛΟΥ Χ
ΑΙΓΕΙΩΝ
ΠΟΔΩΝΤΕΤΤΑ
ΡΩΝ Χ
ΚΕ ΦΑΛΗΣ ―Χ
ΕΝΚΕΦΑΛΟΥΧ
ΜΗΤΡΑ ΣΗΜΝΑ
ΥΘΑΤΙΟΥΗΜΝΑ
ΙΣΟΚΡΕΩΣ
ΗΠΑΤΙΟΥΗΜΝΑ
ΙΣΟΚΡΕΩΣ
ΠΛΕΥΜΟΝΙΟΥ
ΗΜΝΑΕΞΗΜΙΣΟΥΣ
ΒΟΕΙΟΥΠΟΔΟΣ
ΗΠΑΤΟΣΚΑΙΣΠΛΗ
ΝΟΣΗΜΝΑΙΣΟΚΡΕΩΣ
ΠΛΕΥΜΟΝΟΣΗΜΝΑ
ΕΞΗΜΙΣΟΥΣ
ΕΝΚΕΦΑΛΟΥ

The agoranomic inscription from Piraeus.

of the Archaic and Classical foot – used to calculate the *pechys, spithame* and *orgyia*. The second, which is rendered as the sole of a foot, is the length of the Hellenistic foot (0.301 m.). There is another metrological relief in the Ashmolean Museum, Oxford, though this latter is probably a dedication.[4]

To the left is an **agoranomic inscription relating to market control (no. 4628),** which is of interest for the information it supplies about the cost of living and gastronomic habits of the inhabitants of Piraeus in the 1st c. BC. It contains a list of the maximum prices of goods on offer in ancient *ephthopolia* (dressed-meat shops), consisting of legs *(podes)*, "heads" *(kephale ton oston)*, brains *(enkephalos)*, pig's matrix *(metra)*, udder *(outhatios)*, liver *(hepation)*, spleen *(splen)*, lungs *(pleumonion)* and entrails *(cholikia)*. The items on sale are divided into three categories according to quality: first come pork products, followed by goat and lamb, and finally beef. Prices are given for quantities of half a kilogram *(mna)*, in *chalkoi* (one eighth of an obol), or in terms of the price of good-quality meat. The inscription was destroyed in 86 BC when Piraeus was captured by Sulla, and re-engraved in 83 BC by the *Piraeus market inspector (agoranomos tou Peiraios)*.[5]

Next to the inscription, at the entrance to the Cybele room, is a **device (nos. 168+169)** with a series of hollows *(sekomata)* corresponding to different quantities of volume *(kyathon, oxybaphon, hemikotylion, etc.)*, used to check sales of liquids.

The large wall-case opposite the staircase, which contains finds from a number of sanctuaries in Attica dating from the 8th to the 4th c. BC, serves as a prelude to the room devoted to pottery and private life and the Cybele room, opposite and to the right, respectively, of the visitor. In the left part of this case are displayed iron weapons (spearheads, swords), razors, and vessels used in sacrifices, such as cauldrons and spits for roasting the sacrificial victims; they come from the altar of Zeus on the summit of Mount Parnitha (Corinthian pottery of the 7th c. BC).[6] In the top centre of the case are busts, and in the middle, figurines of seated and standing female figures from Attic sanctuaries and graves dating from the 8th c. BC (figurine of a seated deity with a

Measure for liquid volumes.

horse painted on the back of the throne, from Kallithea) to the 4th c. BC. An important exhibit in this case is the terracotta Late Archaic head of a female deity from a small sanctuary in the deme of Aixonides Halai. The bottom shelf contains figurines of deities from various sanctuaries in Piraeus and Attica. At the right are dedications from the Piraeus sanctuary of Artemis Munychia. Pottery from the Middle Bronze Age to the Hellenistic period. The figurines of children are connected with the role of Artemis as *kourotrophos* (nurse). Pottery characteristic of the cult of Munychia includes the krateriskoi with running female figures, also known from the sanctuary at Brauron.[7]

A separate case to the right of the entrance to the pottery room is devoted exclusively to finds **from the Minoan (MM III-LM I) peak sanctuary of Ayios Georgios on Kythera.** This is the first such peak sanctuary to be found outside Crete (excavated by Yannis Sakellarakis in 1992-1993). The sanctuary belonged to a Minoan trading colony, long known on the site of the ancient harbour of Skandeia. There is an impressively large number of finds, most of them belonging to two types. They consist of bronze figurines of male and (more rarely) female adorants with their right hand held to their forehead, or less commonly with both hands on their breast, crossed, or touching their head. Amongst them are parts of larger figurines of high-quality art.

The bronze cutout votive limbs (legs, an arm) are outstanding items, as are the bronze scorpion and the extremely rare votive figure of a woman. There are also *ex voto* weapons and jewellery. Finds of great importance for Minoan religion include the miniature terracotta horns of consecration and a small votive bronze double axe. The most important exhibit is an intact 'spoon' of black steatite inscribed with a Linear A inscription.[8]

In front of the entrance to the room with the funerary monuments is displayed a wooden coffin, a rare find from a 4th c. BC grave at Aigaleo.

ROOM 2

Pottery and small finds from the Mycenaean to the Hellenistic period (1500-300 BC)

The large showcase on the left side of the room contains a selection of pottery and small finds from Piraeus, Kallithea, Tavros, Salamis, Methana and the coastal municipalities from Glyphada to Varkiza. The display is completed by a selection of artefacts (pottery and small finds) from the Meletopoulos-Nomidis Collection and, above all, from the Yeroulanos Collection, the latter coming almost exclusively from the family estate at Trachones. The display follows chronological order. Beginning at the left of the entrance, there is a collection of characteristic pottery from Mycenaean (LH IIIA-C) tombs on Salamis (in the centre, a krater with a depiction of a chariot) (**pl. 3**), jewellery (necklaces) and figurines of the characteristic Mycenaean Φ and Ψ types.[9] The finds in the centre of the case from the recently excavated Mycenaean (LH IIIA/B) sanctuary at Ayios Konstantinos, Methana, are of interest for their rarity, even uniqueness. A selection is displayed of the roughly 150 figurines found on and next to a built bench in the corner of a room in the sanctuary. At the top is a row of four horsemen wearing conical hats (*piloi*) or helmets, between two miniature tripod altars (with applied animal figurines) and a throne. In the centre of the middle row is a very rare depiction of a bull-leaper and a selection of richly, partly naturalistically decorated figurines of a chariot with a pair of deities, or figurines of the so-called 'plough' type, and finally a small selection of the numerous and varied dedications of bovines. The figurines are flanked at left and right by cult vessels from the sanctuary, amongst which are a relief vase with the figure of a bird, and a rhyton in the shape of a pig's head – a rare example of this kind of zoomorphic rhyton from Mycenaean Greece (14th-12th c. BC). The other half of the case is occupied by vases from

Mycenaean tombs (LH IIA/B-LH IIIC) at Voula and Varkiza.10 The rendering of the human figure on the body of the little jug **no. 5131** is interesting.

The objects displayed in the corner of the case are representative of the following, Geometric period. At the left are Protogeometric and Early Geometric (Severe Style) vases from tombs on Salamis. The spindlewhorls with engraved decoration and the two gold pins are from the same cemetery. The interment of the dead man's weapon, in this case a sword, which is wrapped around the neck of the cinerary amphora **no. 6358,** is a burial practice characteristic of the period. At the right is a gold funeral diadem from Anavyssos and a selection of pottery of the mature and late Geometric period (800-700 BC). The precision of the figures and the harmony of Geometric decoration between the figures and the shape of the vase contrasts strongly with the painterly intent (see e.g. the alternating use of black and white in the decoration), the free drawing, and the loose disposition of figures in the large (0.96 m. high) Late Geometric (c. 700 BC) pithamphora **no. 7352** from Trachones at the centre of the case. This is presumably the product of a local workshop. The figures of the horses on the pithamphora and the bird adorning the neck of the amphora **no. 7349** in the same case provide the upper and lower termini, respectively, of the early Archaic or Protoattic period (700-640 BC). This period is represented in the exhibition by three more vases, two krateriskoi from Petralona **(nos. 3432-3433)**[11] and a small amphora **(no. 4254)**, which are displayed in the adjacent case (on the top and bottom shelf). During this period Corinthian pottery made its presence felt everywhere, even inside Attica. A number of examples are displayed on the bottom shelf and there are many more, from the sanctuary on Mount Parnitha, in the showcase in room 1. In the amphora **no. 7348** at the centre, with pairs of panthers and sphinxes, dating from the beginning of the Archaic period proper (6th c. BC), the dynamic power of the figures of the 7th c. has now receded. Their

Protogeometric funerary amphora with the sword of the dead man.

degeneration into blind imitations of the purely decorative Corinthian pottery is marked by the Corinthian fashion of zones of animals and monsters (usually sphinxes) and rich incised decoration, represented here by a vase by the Polos Painter, **no. 7037** (bottom shelf).

The zenith of Attic pottery is associated with two styles of figure-rendering, known as the black-figure (down to about the end of the 6th c. BC) and the red-figure (from 520 to the 4th c. BC) styles. The skyphos **no. 831** with a depiction of Herakles and the fragment **no. 6948** next to it belong to the mature Archaic art of the middle of the 6th c. BC, in which the black paint is given added brilliance by the addition of purple or white. The shapes of the vases, as well as the figures, are solid and robust, as in the skyphos just mentioned. A good idea of the development of the style can be derived from comparison of contemporary lekythoi with those of the middle of the 5th c. BC. The earlier type, **no. 6467** (middle shelf) with the depiction of a Siren, still has the oval body of its Corinthian precursors. Amongst the later black-figure lekythoi with added white (early 5th c. BC), particular interest attaches to the iconography of **no. 7339** from Kallithea, with a depiction of a goat sacrifice. By contrast, the large number of contemporary, smaller lekythoi (bottom shelf) were mass-produced. The black-figure technique survives in these, normally in mythological scenes (labours of Herakles, chariots, a banquet, Dionysiac scenes) that are difficult to interpret on account of the poor-quality drawing, or in purely decorative motifs (palmettes, ivy leaves).

The vases with red-figure decoration on display cover the period from the middle of the 5th to about the middle of the 4th c. BC. Outstanding amongst them are: the hydria **no. 3031**, still in the Severe Style, with a depiction of Zeus pursuing a nymph; the bowl **no. 6837** from Voula, the interior of which is decorated with a representation of a troupe of sea deities, Nereus and the Nereids, carrying the weapons of Achilles; a series of vases, most of them loutrophoroi, with wedding scenes, the finest of which is the loutrophoros **no. 7345 (pl. 4),** from the Yeroulanos Collection; red-figure lekythoi with funeral scenes (dead hoplite **no. 3214,** youth seated in front of a grave stele, **no. 6733**); the fragment of an oinochoe, **no. 7443,** with a banquet scene (a banqueter playing kottabos); and smaller vases, mainly aryballoid lekythoi, with figures of Victory and Eros, sitting tranquilly or pursuing girls and young men. The large amphora **no. 7341 (pl. 5)** from Trachones, the ancient deme of Euonymon, is by the Dinos Painter. It has a representation of the collection of oil from the sacred olives of Attica, the Moriai, attended by the goddess Athena herself. The oil was kept for three years before being awarded as the prize in the Panathenaic games in special vases called Panathenaic amphoras. The depiction of an amphora in the scene suggests that this vase was probably one of those actually used for this purpose. The depiction on the back, showing Demeter, Kore and Pluto, patron deities of farming, completes the peaceful picture of rural Attica and was entirely appropriate to the period of the Peace of Nikias, to which the vase should be dated. On the bottom shelf are examples of Classical glass vases. The type of the white funerary lekythos with a multicoloured scene is represented here by an example from Salamis, **no. 6560,** of very impressive size and dating from the last quarter of the 5th c. BC. From the 4th c. BC date the globular pelike **no. 7484** with a Dionysiac scene, found during the recent excavations for the new motorway in Attica at Kantza, and (below) the stand of a nuptial lebes from Trachones **no. 7346,** with bare-breasted girls dancing around an incense-burner to the sound of the lyre.[12] The display closes with a selection from the large collection of black-glaze amphoras (and also a lamp) in the museum. This austere technique, which was used alongside the red-figure style until it supplanted it completely in the Hellenistic period, essentially abandons all pretence at decoration. The only exceptions before the Hellenistic period are the stamped palmettes and circles found inside skyphoi, or the fluting on the exterior of large vases. The sole expressive means of this pottery are the precision and aesthetic perfection of the form of the vase itself, which now vies with metal vases, a few examples of which can be seen in the case opposite.

Everyday life and art in the Classical period

The right part of the room, as we enter from the vestibule, is occupied by a large case containing objects illustrating private life in Attica from the Archaic to the Hellenistic period.

The charming **world of the child,** to which the first part of the display is devoted, is illustrated by a series of grave groups from children's tombs dating from the 6th to the 4th c. BC. These are normally miniature vases which, like modern toys, are exact imitations of real pottery, with fine decoration. Other children's objects are displayed, such as feeding bottles, rattles (bottom shelf, left), dolls **(pl. 6)** and terracotta animals, a child's iron strigil and astragaloi (knuckle-bones), and an alphabet scratched on a potsherd. A common find in children's tombs consisted of the special vases given to children at the festival of the Anthesteria; these were small oinochoai *(choai)* with representations of children at play. The second section introduces the visitor, through a few selected vases and vessels, to the world of the **women's quarters,** which combines the peace and familiarity of these apartments with everyday activity in the kitchen and at the loom. The atmosphere of the boudoir, and especially the ritual of make-up, is recalled by vases of various shapes and decoration: red-figure or marble pyxides, perfume containers (lekythoi and alabastra), and above all by mirrors, one of which **(no. 7986)** is a folding mirror with a depiction of Aphrodite Epitragia from a tomb at Moschato. The scenes decorating the walls of the vases offer a fleeting glimpse inside this world, in which we see a woman looking at herself in a mirror, in a rare depiction of the image of a face (alabastron **no. 6255** from Ilioupoli, c. 500 BC); women are

Offerings from children's graves of the 4th (above) and 5th (below) c. BC.

also represented, normally on nuptial lebetes, sitting in their room and receiving wedding presents. The central position occupied in a woman's life by her daily involvement with household chores is illustrated by the cooking vessels on display (bottom shelf, bowl, cooking pot, saucepan, frying pan), by scenes of women carrying water from a spring, spinning or weaving, and finally by actual vessels, such as the epinetron or onos **no. 7353** (a semicylindrical vessel to protect the woman's thigh from the distaff as she spun), the spindlewhorl, and the primitive loom (in which the warp threads are not attached to the frame but hang separately with the aid of special conical loomweights). This picture of the woman's world is completed by a row of figurines of elegant ladies, at the top, and the less elegant, but typologically very interesting, squatting naked woman (**pl. 7**), a parody of the famous Aphrodite by the sculptor Doidalsas executed in the middle of the 3rd c. BC (**no. 4834**). In the centre is a nuptial lebes of the 4th c. BC (**no. 7187**) in which the female body is again rendered with added white paint, as in the Archaic period.

In the central section of the case are displayed the finds from **the 'tomb of the poet' at Daphne.** The musical instruments he used – the triangle, a form of harp (in the centre), the lyre, of which all that survives is the tortoise shell that served as a sound-box, and the pipe – seem to have been made by the poet himself, as is evident from the saw that accompanied him in his grave. He also wrote the words of his songs. His bronze pencil-holder and iron eraser were found in a wooden pencil-case. Five wax-coated wooden tablets, which were originally bound together in a book, were also found, with barely distinguishable letters on the wax, as well as a papyrus, unfortunately badly damaged. Next to these is an earlier red-figure lekythos, **no. BK 1990,** with a depiction of Apollo, patron god of poets, with the lyre.

The centre of the third part of the case is dedicated to the **masculine world.** The life of Athenian youths was closely bound up with the *gymnasium*. The objects that accompanied the athlete to the grave were the strigil, which he used after wrestling to clean the sand of the palaestra from his oiled body, and sometimes the *aryballos*, a small vase containing the oil, or the arytaina *(ladle)* to draw the oil from the pithos owned by the gymnasium. Possibly the supreme duty and greatest honour for a citizen was to take part as a hoplite in the most important, military, conflicts involving his city. This predominantly male world is reflected in the two Archaic helmets, a Corinthian helmet of the 7th c. BC **(pl. 8)** and a Chalkidian helmet of the 6th c. BC **(pl. 9),** and also in the bronze spearhead at the centre of the case. A picture of a hoplite is provided by the Archaic stele from Troizen. As in the 'female' case, the picture is supplemented by a series of figurines and vase-paintings, mainly of young athletes (the depiction of the victor in a torch-race on the small trefoil oinochoe **no. 4344** is particularly interesting) and hoplites, though there are also scenes referring to more humble professions, such as the red-figure lekythos **no. 7073** with the rare depiction of a wood-cutter or possibly a fighter felling an olive tree **(pl. 10).** Objects connected with work, fishing equipment, and medical implements are less important in terms of visual interest, but they are nevertheless characterised by a certain functional elegance (bottom right of the central case). At the bottom of this same case is displayed a cinerary urn (a vase containing cremated ashes) engraved with the name of the dead person.

A bronze cinerary urn at the bottom of the last section of the case, next to the entrance, and a selection of various bronze vases, including a jug, a small krater and bowls with bosses, from graves at Troizen, serve to mark the transition to the next room, which houses the bronzes. One interesting grave yielded the objects displayed on the top shelf in the case, on which items classically associated with athletes, such as the strigil and the ladle, are exhibited alongside objects connected with female beautification, such as an alabaster pyxis, an elegant little kylix, little mirrors, and an amulet of rock crystal. From the same grave comes the 'Melian' relief **(pl. 11)** with a scene of Herakles killing the Centaur Nessos, a rare item in the display (ca. 460 BC).

Figurine of Eros.

THE BRONZE STATUES OF PIRAEUS

The four bronze statues and the tragic mask displayed in rooms 3 and 4 were discovered in the summer of 1959, together with three marble pieces (two hermaic stelai and a marble statuette of an oriental Artemis in the Cybele room), during work on the drains at the corner of Vasileos Georgiou Protou and Philonos Streets, behind the Tinaneios garden. It was evident from the way they had been placed and the position in which they were found that they had been stored in a room in the harbour, possibly in 87 BC, to prevent them from being carried off, and were then buried when the storehouse was destroyed by fire. Soon after their discovery, the bronzes were taken to the National Archaeological Museum in Athens for conservation, and remained there until 1983, when they returned to the Piraeus Museum.

The sculptures are some of the very few – about 35 in all – large-scale bronze statues of all periods to survive anywhere in the world. The Piraeus bronzes come from the world of great art. In them is expressed, in a more profound, more clearly sculptural language, the same message transmitted to us in lower tones by the humble grave stelai in the Museum.[13]

ROOM 3

Archaic sculpture – the bronze Apollo of Piraeus

The **Piraeus Apollo no. 4645 (pl. 12)** is the only surviving bronze kouros, and at the same time the earliest cast Greek statue. The walls of the statue are still very thick, and parts of the clay core and the iron frame were found inside it. The god it depicts can immediately be recognised from his external divine emblems, the bow and the bowl – probably made of gold – traces of which can be detected on his hands; the bronze technique means that the arms do not hang completely free of the sides of the body. The fact that the right leg is advanced, in contrast with the normal schema for a kouros, is probably to be explained by the presence of Leto or Artemis next to him in the same group. At a more profound level, however, the identification of the god is based on the ethos of the figure.

Taking as its starting point the world of the palaestra, the sculptured figure of the kouros was formed during the Late Archaic period into the types of the athlete, the hero and the god, thanks to fine distinctions in the form of the body, the posture and the style. In chronological terms, the Apollo lies towards the end of the one hundred years of development of the kouros, which begins with superb symbols of youth at the end of the 7th century, such as the statues of Kleobis and Biton at Delphi. The Apollo is slightly later than the young aristocrats made in the great decade of Archaic sculpture, 530-520 BC, like the Kroisos of Anavyssos, whose bodies are robust, fit, and lit up by their confident smiles. The stance of the Apollo reveals a tendency to emancipation from the form of the kouros and the tyranny of the vertical axis. The weight is no longer distributed equally between the legs: the transfer of the weight to the right leg is achieved organically, but it is mainly through the modelling of these superb limbs that it becomes clear that they are now really bearing the weight of the body. The slight forward inclination and turn to the right that can be detected in the coiffure, and the lack of symmetry of the face and torso, suggest that the god's movement and attention are concentrated on the right side, on which he is holding out the bowl and pouring a libation. The introspective nature of the figure, the serious expression in the long, stern face, in which the axes are emphasised, the high forehead crowned by two pairs of volute tresses, rather like an Ionic capital, suggest that the statue, in both ethos and stance, is the predecessor of the Cassel Apollo. Like any original work of art, the Piraeus Apollo fills the spectator with wonder, though this is accompanied by bafflement as to its date and the workshop that produced it. The contrast between the severe facial features and the rich modelling of the body has suggested various interpretations: for some, it is a Late Archaic work inspired by an earlier cult statue, probably from a Boeotian workshop, while others associate it with the affected Archaising current in the Late Hellenistic period – though this last view is based on the erroneous statement that Hellenistic sherds were found in its clay core.[14]

Opposite the bronze Apollo are displayed two more Archaic sculptures. It is interesting to compare him with the statuette of an Archaic kouros, made of Parian marble and found in the German excavations of the temple of Aphaia on Aegina, a fine example of Archaic sculpture (despite the destruction of the larger part of the face) and a pioneering work from the great Aeginetan workshop. The kouros is dated to just before the middle of the 6th c. BC. It is on temporary exhibition here until the museum on Aegina is completed.[15] The only Archaic female statue in the museum is the statuette **no. 2530** of an early Archaic kore (ca. 580 BC), worked in a cylindrical sculptural type known mainly from Samos. It was found in a rubbish dump at Ayios Ioannis Rendis, and it is not known, therefore, whether it was a dedication from a sanctuary or a funerary statue.[16]

Archaic Kore from Ayios Ioannis Rendis, Athens.

ROOM 4

Bronze statues of the 4th c. BC

The other three statues take us to a radically different world. The spare, powerful sculptural language of the Archaic youths moves us more fruitfully, and speaks more directly to our soul and senses than the goddesses of the 4th c. BC in the room we now enter. These are figures that centuries of Classicism have reduced to empty stereotypes. In them can be seen not only the perfecting of the 5th c. BC Classical figure, which is beginning to emerge in the Apollo, but also the even more astonishing change in the general perception of the figure that marks the transition from the 5th to the 4th c. BC. The work of sculpture (whether statue or, as we shall see in the following rooms, relief) is no longer perceived as autonomous, but invariably in relation to its natural or transcendental environment. Movement, turn, expression and direction of gaze are all deployed in 4th c. BC statues to create an imaginary space around them and a specific relationship with the worshipper or spectator. The figure now functions as a picture, and the interest is therefore concentrated on the front side, which is the only angle from which its plasticity can be perceived. At the same time, there is a change in the perception of the god. The daemonic figures of the 6th c. BC and the transcendental ones of the 5th c. BC now give way to the very human deities of the 4th c. BC. Characteristic here is the triumphant advance of Asklepios, who either supplants Zeus or exercises an influence on the iconography of his figure. So the three goddesses in this room, sealed in their own emotional world, motionless in a timeless stance, stoop compassionately towards the spectator, extending their hand with the bowl.

The large Artemis no. 4647, the first statue in this room (pl. 13), was from the very beginning the subject of long debate, centring both on its interpretation and date, and on its attribution to one of the great sculptors of the 4th c. BC. The sturdy young woman, who has the characteristic hairstyle with the tresses arranged radially in what is known to archaeologists as the 'melon coiffure' *(Melonenfrisur)* has been identified by some, on the strength of the similarity with known heads of Sappho, as a poetess or Muse. This identification seemed to be confirmed by the tragic mask **(pl. 14)** that accompanied it. In fact, however, it is Artemis, who can be recognised not so much from the style of the figure, for which there are several parallels, such as the Dresden Artemis, as from the details: the traces of the quiver-support on her back, and the position of the fingers of her left hand, which was holding the bow. The treatment of the body and drapery, which has clear references to the (marble) Apollo Patroös from the Agora, suggest that this statue should be probably be attributed to Euphranor. Euphranor, a sculptor and painter, was the main representative of the Classical current in the middle of the 4th c. BC, and sought a return to more robust, earthly figures with Classical proportions. As Euphranor himself said, his own Theseus was reared on meat, while that of Parrhasios was brought up on roses. The rather theatrical frontality of this work, which is evident also in the neglect of the rear, and the excessive emphasis placed on the diagonal contrasts of the figure, have in the past suggested that this statue, too, should be assigned to one of the Classicising phases of Hellenistic sculpture. This, however, is ruled out not so much by the association with Euphranor as by the high quality of the piece.[17]

The statuette of the **small Artemis, no. 4648 (pl. 15)** comes from a different iconographic tradition. The sculptural type known from Attic reliefs dating from the second half of the 4th c. BC is much closer to the Classical perception of the virgin goddess of the hunt. The body is slender, virgin, almost boyish, and the impression of youth is further emphasised by a certain instability in the stance deriving from the general turn of the figure towards the relaxed leg (turn of the head, position of the arm). She wears an Attic peplos (with the belt above the overfall), here girt high, and a himation wrapped around her shoulders and tucked into the belt to make it easier to move. The head is small, with clearly delineated, almost severe, facial features, and the hair is gathered in a bun at the front, called the lampadion. The severe treatment of the drapery, the fact that the figure tapers towards the top, the high belt, and the small head are all elements that emphasise the vertical axis, which is interrupted only by the double horizontal line of the hem of the overfall. All this gives the figure the appearance of a column, and dates the statuette fairly late in the 4th c. BC. The workmanship is meticulous, with many of the details inlaid (baldric, sandals), and if the piece had not been so badly affected by oxidisation, it would be the pride of this room.

The larger than life size **Athena, no. 4646** appears at first sight to be the earliest of the three works. However, despite its resemblance to the Athena Parthenos, there is no surviving trace in it of the majesty of the Pheidian model. The resemblance to the posture and drapery of the well-known, accurately dated work by Kephisodotos, the Eirene of 375 BC, is equally superficial. For all this, it must have been a famous work, as is shown by a Roman variant with the right hand supported on the waist – the Mattei Athena in the Louvre. Athena's head is covered by a Corinthian helmet adorned with owls and griffins, with a crest supported on a snake. Athena is dressed in a peplos, plainly girt with no pouch *(kolpos)*. The overfall hangs obliquely down to the middle of the left thigh and is pulled up at the back to serve as a head-cover, as commonly found in ancient depictions of women. The right leg, on which the weight rests heavily, is emphasised by three groups of vertical folds in the garment, and the relaxed leg is drawn languidly behind. The oblique drapery of the overfall, and the shield, also set obliquely, shift the rocking movement of the statue to the right, where it culminates in the turn and tilt of the head towards the right arm, which was holding Victory. The left arm hangs down and, as the position of the fingers shows, would have supported the shield and spear. Athena nonetheless lacks the robustness of the statues of the period of the Eirene, and even of Classicising works dating from the middle of the 4th c. BC, such as the Apollo Patroös by Euphranor (to whom this piece has been attributed), or the large Artemis from Piraeus contemporary with it. In contrast with the dynamic juxtaposition of folds, as clear as the flutes of a column, which support that figure, sharing the weight with the left leg, which is drawn behind, the movement and drapery of the Athena are characterised by a distinct lack of dynamism and reveal a weariness that, in the relatively small face, takes the form of a sugary sentimentalism. The statue cannot, therefore, be dated earlier than the end of the 4th c. BC, and, judging by the form of the sandals, could be a Hellenistic work.[18]

A separate showcase is devoted to parts of the bronze sheathing of a shield decorated with a relief quadriga. The shield, which was found together with the bronze statues, does not belong to the Athena.

The dating of the Piraeus find to the time of the siege by Sulla, on the basis of a coin found during the excavation, the fact that the statues were buried after a fire connected with the destruction of the city by the Roman dictator, and finally the circumstance that the find includes four cult statues, one of Apollo and two of Artemis (three if account is taken of the marble figure of an oriental Artemis), are all supporting evidence for the hypothesis advanced by George Dontas: that the statues were brought to Piraeus from Delos for safekeeping after the sanctuary there had been plundered by Mithridates' general. The fact that they were buried would indeed be surprising if they had formed part of Sulla's booty.

Bronze statue of Athena (height 2.35 m.).

Two hermaic stelai,
1st c. BC.

The temple with the cult statue of the Mother of the Gods, from Moschato.

ROOM 5

The sanctuary of the Mother of the Gods (Cybele) at Moschato. Reconstruction of an ancient sanctuary

The two hermaic stelai **nos. 3858 and 3859,** dating from the 1st c. BC, which stand at the entrance to this room, were found together with the bronze statues. They are fine examples of a well-known type of stele that was used as a boundary marker for private, public (stoas, gymnasia) and sacred areas. The head reproduces the original Archaistic type of the (bearded) Hermes that was created by Alkamenes, the pupil of Pheidias. The rectangular stele with the inset male member (missing) and the horizontal beam was a kind of aniconic depiction of the deity.

The room itself has been laid out as a typical ancient sanctuary. The main elements in the reconstruction – the temple, altar, votive reliefs and perirrhanterion – come from various sanctuaries of Piraeus and the surrounding municipalities. The kernel of it consists of the small temple with the cult statue of Cybele, Mother of the Gods, **no. 3851,** which was found at Moschato, at the junction between Thermopylon and Xenophontos Streets, near the church of the Metamorphosis. The temple itself is still preserved *in situ* and the one in the museum is an exact copy. The cult statue of the enthroned goddess (which had an inset head that has not been found) is the finest, and the only Classical (4th c. BC), copy of the 'Pheidian' Mother of the Gods attributed to Agorakritos, The goddess had her left hand on the drum, and held a bowl in her right. Her inseparable companion, the lion, sat next to her on a separate base.[19] Small temples, or naïskoi, of Cybele constituted a type of votive relief that was very widely found throughout the Greek world from as early as the Archaic period; the examples arranged to right and left of the temple and at the back of the room come from the Metroön in the Piraeus. This sanctuary, which is known from the literary sources, was excavated in the middle of the 19th century by the French occupation army, who did not record its location. The naïskoi also come from Roman houses excavated in Piraeus, where the goddess seems to have occupied an important position in domestic worship. Two basic types of the seated Cybele can be distinguished: the type created by Agorakritos and another, later type of a high-girded figure. The lion occupies a different position in each type, which is either held by the goddess on her knees or is next to her. The antae of some of the naïskoi are carved with relief figures of the goddess's attendants: a woman holding torches (in the type of Artemis Phosphoros) and a youth wearing a chlamys, or, more rarely, Pan. A picture of a sanctuary of the Mother of the Gods is provided by the votive relief **no. 1165** (inscription: κράτους Μητρί Θεῶν ἀνέθεσαν: dedicated to the Mother of the Gods): in front of the worshipper is depicted a low hearth and a naïskos of Cybele, above which, in a separate panel can be seen the heads of the goddess's followers, two Nymphs and three armed Kouretes.[20]

Beneath the windows in this room are displayed some of the finest votive reliefs in the museum's collection. The first, **no. 405 (pl. 16)** comes from the Asklepieion and dates from the last years of the 5th c. BC when, as we know from Aristophanes, the sanctuary was flourishing. Sick people used to lie in a stoa in the sanctuary (at Epidauros, the abaton), and would see the god in their sleep, who explained to them how to recover their health. A healing of this kind is depicted here. Asklepios stoops and puts his hands on the patient. Behind the god stands his daughter Hygieia, and opposite him are the relatives who dedicated the relief. The second and third reliefs are amongst the earliest and finest examples of a type of heroic relief known as the 'funeral banquet', in which heroes, or dead persons heroised after their death, are shown participating in an eternal divine banquet, indicated by the couch and the small table next to it. The first of the two, **no. 1178,** is in the Rich Style: the reclining hero holds a bowl, and his wife, Heroine, sits at his feet.[21] The second, **no. 208,** is slightly later and reproduces the type more accurately, with the addition of a young cup-bearer opposite Heroine. The other sculptures in the room move in less elevated tones. To the left of the entrance from the Apollo room is the small relief **no. 211,** dedicated by Pythonikos in fulfilment of a vow to the *Agathe Thea* (Good Goddess), who is depicted wearing a polos and holding a cornucopia in her right hand; behind her hangs a model of a leg, the object of the vow. At the top is the inscription *'To the Good Goddess, Pythonikos, having prayed, dedicated'*. At the right, between the two entrances, are dedications to Artemis. The only statue found in the sanctuary of Artemis Munychia, **no. 1927**, is also displayed here. It is an Archaistic female torso with a torch in the left hand, and is presumably a statue of Artemis Phosphoros dating from the period when the sanctuary was in decline, in the 2nd c. BC. Next to it is the marble, column-like statuette of a female figure, **no. 3857,** found with the Piraeus bronzes, which has post-Praxitelean facial features. The distinctive style of dress (specifically, the manner in which it is girt) enables us to recognise a figure of Artemis from south-west Asia Minor – Artemis Kindyas.[22] Relief **no. 5785** is a chance find from Galatsi, Athens, and was dedicated to the Apollonian Trinity: from the left, Leto, Artemis and Apollo kitharodos in front of an altar. The figures of the gods imitate known models of the 4th c. BC. To the left of the door from the vestibule are various reliefs from Piraeus. They are dedicated to Herakles, who is receiving a sacrifice **(no. 33),** and to a hero horseman **(no. 2041),** which is considerably damaged by its exposure to the sea. Finally, relief **no. 10,** has an enthroned figure in the type of Zeus, with his right hand resting high on his sceptre; behind him are carved wreaths – two columns of five wreaths at the front and one column of four wreaths at the back – with traces of later carving.

The reconstruction of the sanctuary is completed by two more exhibits that formed essential features of every ancient sanctuary. The monolithic altar **no. 3583** displayed opposite the entrance to the temple has a much later inscription to Helios (Mithras), whose cult flourished greatly in the 3rd c. AD. In contrast, the perirrhanterion that held purification water at the entrance to a sanctuary is dated to the late 6th c. BC by the Archaic votive inscription on the rim of the bowl.

The votive relief of Pythonikos dedicated to the Agathe Thea (Good Goddess).

Archaising state of Artemis Phosphoros from the sanctuary at Munychia. 2nd c. BC.

Votive relief to an unknown hero (funeral banquet).

ROOM 6

Grave stelai 420-350 BC

The history of Classical grave reliefs as seen through the rooms of the Piraeus Museum

The Piraeus Museum house a collection of 5th and 4th century grave reliefs that is unique in terms of both quality and quantity. Grave reliefs were a fundamental way of giving aesthetic expression to ancient Athenian beliefs relating to life and death. Visitors can form a clear picture of the wealth of the repertoire and follow the development of the relief through well-known examples, beginning with its birth in the workshops created on the Acropolis centred on Pheidias and his pupils, and ending abruptly in 317 BC.[23]

The room containing reliefs of the first period (420-350 BC) is pervaded by a sense of the peaceful acceptance of the death of a youth, a young woman, or a mother who died in childbirth. The grave reliefs of metics accompanied by Phoenician inscriptions reflects the composition of the population of Piraeus.

The repertoire of Classical grave reliefs

The grave marker – a plain or relief stele, a slab, or a statue marking the resting place of the deceased – was associated with people's innermost fears and the profound hope of transcending death, and was one of the earliest forms of art. In the Archaic period (7th and 6th c. BC) the funerary monument enjoyed an unprecedented flowering, taking the form of a stele usually surmounted by a Sphinx (a protective daemon from the underworld), or by a statue of the young man or woman. This aristocratic art came to a sudden end when such provocative displays of luxury were banned by the democracy newly founded by Kleisthenes in 510 BC.

Wealth had to be accumulated from the members of the Athenian Confederacy, and a new generation of sculptors had to emerge around the workshops of the Parthenon before the grave relief could make a fresh start. The Classical relief differs from the Archaic both morphologically and in terms of its iconography and its narrative content. Alongside the tall stele topped by a palmette, which retained the form and decoration of the Archaic grave marker, a broader type of slab, which provided space for a narrative scene related to the deceased, became increasingly important. Iconographically, the predominant scene is a farewell scene, a scene of *dexiosis* (handshake); this was a tranquil scene in which the living members of the family are found together with the dead, with no anguish or lamentation, all of them meeting in a common place beyond life and death. As in the Archaic period, the finest reliefs are devoted to those who died young, since it was the death of a young man, normally depicted as an athlete (**no. 13**) and more rarely as a hoplite (**no. 1201**), that shocked the family more than anything else. Alongside the characteristic Greek sense of youthful beauty, which found an occasion for expression in these monuments, the presence of women becomes increasingly apparent. The woman is depicted as a child playing with her doll (**no. 1703**) or domestic pet, such as a goose or puppy (**no. 264**), or as a young woman shut up in her own daily world, indicated by the basket of wool under her chair (**no. 3581**), or brought by a maidservant (**no. 5290**) or looking at herself in the mirror (**nos. 28, 34**), or bedecking herself with the assistance of the maidservant who is holding a jewellery box, a band, or a piece of jewellery (**no. 2555**). More commonly, the woman sits and receives her husband's greeting (**no. 259**) or that of a relative (**no. 2152**).

Childbirth, the cause of so many female deaths, and a common phenomenon until the modern age, is seldom represented; depictions of

Grave relief of a woman with a basket, no. 5290.

1. The funerary lekythos of 'Nikostrate, good wife'.

2. Funerary lekythos with a scene of a visit to the tomb.

3. The grave stele of Eirene of Byzantium.

death, indeed, are generally rare in ancient art or tragedy. Occasionally, however, there is a clear reference, in the image of the maidservant holding the newly born child, as in the stele of Eirene of Byzantium, **no. 3582,** or the neglected appearance of the young mother looking at herself in the mirror for the last time, and the despairing movement of the child next to her on the marble lekythos **no. 34.** The depiction of the grave itself is rare in reliefs though common in white-ground lekythoi; it is found, for example in the marble lekythos **no. 1700,** on which the dead woman sits on the ground at the foot of the monument and receives a visit from a relative, attended by her maidservant. The monument acquires particular interest from a technical detail: the inset stele (N. Zapheiropoulos, *Μαρμάρινη λήκυθος μετ' επιτυμβίου παραστάσεως, Αρχ. Εφημ.* 1953/54 II pp. 237-246).

This anonymous world of relief stelai and marble funerary vases, which imitate the real vases that accompanied the dead to the grave, such as lekythoi and loutrophoroi, reflects, in the tranquillity of death, an entire society of men, women, children, youths, old men, freemen and slaves, citizens and foreigners (especially in the case of Piraeus), who lived in Attica in the 4th c. BC. The stelai of foreign metics are particularly interesting. From inscriptions referring to the foundation of sanctuaries for deities such as the Thracian Bendis, the Egyptian Isis, the Cypriot Aphrodite, or the Phoenician Herakles, we know the origins of a large number of metics who resided here. Two bilingual (Greek and Phoenician) stelai are on display: one is that of Eirene of Byzantium **(no. 3582)** already mentioned **(no. 3580),** and the other is that of a Phoenician metic, the palm-tree *(phoinix)* in the background being a reference to his origins.

The morphological evolution of grave reliefs from 420 to 350 BC

The collection of grave reliefs in the Piraeus Museum provides an exceptionally fine illustration not only of attitudes to life and death, but also of the development of Classical art at the transition from the world of the 5th century to that of the 4th. The series of six very fine reliefs that adorn the two opposite side-walls of the room enables us to follow the gradual freeing of the forms from the stele, which was accompanied by a deepening of the physical and moral (emotional) space of the representation. This development makes clear the turn by art to the individual space and the private character of the monument; this is an example of the general emancipation of the individual from the group that ultimately led to the decline of the ancient city-state and Classical art.

A memory of the tall stele crowned with a palmette and carved with a standing figure of the deceased is preserved, as in the stele of Nikeso **no. 264** (420-410), but the relief figure is already independent of the body of the stele, standing forward and partly covering the palmette. Figure and stele stand in two distinct parallel planes with no internal connection between them. The stele of the two young hoplites Chairedemos and Lykeas **no. 385 (pl. 17),** which was found on Salamis, dates from the time of the Peloponnesian War. Unlike the usual type, the figures here are linked not by a handshake but by their parallel movement to the right. The modelled quality of these statue-like figures is more pronounced than in other contemporary works, in which the outline completely dominates the low relief. The opening up of the figures to the space is also emphasised: although the dressed figure at the back is moving parallel with the surface of the stele, the nude figure, in which the influence of the Peloponnesian type of Polykleitos's Doryphoros is evident, seems to be turned three-quarters away from it. Nevertheless, the parallel arrangement and identical rhythm governing the two figures leaves no margin for independence. The harmonious outline still appears to keep them bound to the slab, of which they are an inseparable part, in precisely the same way that the 5th century BC statue is closed within the specific sculptural space that defines its stance, and that the citizen is confined within the space of the city. Consequently, the stele needs no border.

The same sculptural conception is to be found in the contemporary stele (also from Salamis) with the very rare depiction of an actor gazing intently at a tragic mask that he holds proudly before him, possibly commemorating a theatre success **(pl. 18)**. Only the head of the young man, and the mask, are preserved, and we do not know, therefore, whether the actor was depicted standing or seated, in the type more appropriate to a grave relief.[24]

The dominance of the outline tended to develop into the so-called Rich Style of the end of the century – an artistic manner in which garments, for example, virtually lose their material being and closely follow the calligraphic shapes of the drapery, while at the same time the body essentially becomes weightless. Thus, the young woman looking at herself in the mirror **no. 28,** despite the three-quarters turn of her body, is so effectively enclosed within the outline that she does not really need the support, which is borrowed from its Pheidian sculptural models such as the Aphrodite in the Gardens. Similarly strong Pheidian influence can be seen in the adjacent relief **no. 46,** on the left long side of the room, here in the form of specific recollections of the Parthenon frieze. A link (both aesthetic and emotional) between these figures, closed in their own space, could only be created by subjecting them to a broader harmonious scheme, as in the case of the famous stele of Hegeso from the Kerameikos, now in the National Archaeological Museum of Athens. In the conservative version of this Classical motif to be found on the neighbouring, low flat relief **no 3638,** crowned by an architrave with a palmette and lotus flowers, the only link between the figures is provided by the shared background of the stele.

The first relief on the narrow side of the room opposite is the unfortunately badly mutilated stele of Philo **no. 387;** on this the sculptural approach of the Rich Style finds itself confronted with a new perception, which is on its way to overturning the harmonious, almost beauty-worshipping world of the late 5th c. BC and giving new power to the human figure. When compared with the calligraphic outline that encloses the figure of her young relative – ascending from the back, following the inclination of the head and continuing in the conventional charming gesture – Philo seems to belong to another world. The interest showed in the rendering of the volume and weight of the body, which can be seen in the stance and in the way the head is supported, and the deliberate turn towards the spectator, reveal that solid sculptural values have now replaced the outline as the artist's expressive means. Alongside the increased plasticity of the body forms, the role played by the clothing changes: its relationship to the body becomes more real, and all static, calligraphic forms and fine drapery are abandoned. Clothing no longer slavishly follow the lines of the body, but clings to it here and there, in places revealing its curves and elsewhere apparently reacting to its own weight and emphasising its own sculptural value, as it hangs, stretches or is gathered together, or becomes crumpled. The new corporeal life that animates the figures, blurring the boundary provided by the background, requires that the conventional border be developed in depth, so that it can enclose them within itself. The relief of Philo marks the first appearance of the small temple (naïskos), in this case with Ionic columns, as a border for the representation.

In the adjacent stele of Hippomachos and Kallias **no. 386 (pl. 19),** with a scene of a father bidding farewell to his son, dated to the early 4th c. BC, the figures are now almost totally detached from the stele (as is clear from the left forearm of Hippomachos, which recedes into the background). This causes the background of the stele to retreat; it no longer functions as a simple, tranquil frame for the scene but evolves into an architectural frame for the sculptural figures, which now move in space and lean against the pilasters, beneath the architrave. The growth of the sculptural independence of the figures paves the way for the liberation of individual emotion and internalised movement. The element connecting them is no longer the continuous outline that pinned the figures of the two hoplites Chairedemos and Lykeas to the surface of the slab, in an identical elegiac intent. The link can now be seen to be the result of inner strength. Their movements are pervaded by individual psychological impulses: the slight turn of Hippomachos's head is an expression of the commiseration and grief that we sense to be overwhelming him. In this way, death is made more human and the figures experience it more specifically, as pain and the vacuum created by a final parting. It is to this deepening, this individualisation of the psychological space, that is owed the tender interest in women and children and also the first attempts to render personal features, as in the humble relief **no. 1161,** depicting an old man bidding farewell to his son. The epigram informs us that he lost one son while he was still alive and is himself welcoming the other to Hades (see C.W. Claimont, *Gravestone and Epigram,* 1970, no. 36).

On the stele from Glyphada, **no. 2555 (pl. 20),** one of the most important grave reliefs of the first decade of the 4th c. BC,[25] the Classical figure of the woman taking the necklace from the young maidservant (the play between the arms of the two figures is superb) now resembles a statue worked in the round, though not yet fully independent of the stele.

The parallel development of the sculptural quality of the figures and the architectural border of the relief, described above, formed the prerequisites for the creation of an independent space in which a multifigural representation could freely be developed. The scene of *dexiosis* with several figures set side by side, **no. 209,** still represents the established, linear manner of composition, in the type of the procession of adorants typical of votive reliefs. After the middle

The grave stele of Andron.

of the century, by contrast, there was a tendency towards the creation of semicircular compositions. A third figure, usually rendered frontally, closes the composition in a circle, and replaces the background, which the sculptural quality of the figures had already caused to retreat. The relief of the Megarian athlete Agetor **no. 13** (380-370 BC) marks a step towards the formulation of this type òf circular composition **(pl. 21)**. The figure itself fills the full width of the stele through the semicircular inclination of the body of the athlete scraping himself clean. The impression of instability (physical and emotional) is due to the inability of the outline to contain the fully developed sculptural figure, which attempts to support itself against the pilaster formed by the border.

The deepening of the space in the relief follows the contemporary development in the 4th c. BC of a 'painterly' conception of the work of sculpture. In the statuette **no. 430,** of a boy victor who was holding a strigil,

dating from 400-390 BC (in the middle of the room), the clearly delineated musculature and the diagonally contrasting movement of its 5th-century Polykleitian models recede beneath the gentle chiaroscuro and the almost dreamlike impression created by the slightly turned head, which, like Agetor, gazes uncertainly into space **(pl. 22).**

*Grave stele
no. 209.*

74

GROUND FLOOR

ROOMS 7 and 8

Grave reliefs and funerary monuments 350-307 BC.

In the vestibule on the ground floor (room 7) and the adjacent, specially designed room opposite the entrance to the Museum (room 8), visitors can follow the final chapter in the development of the Classical grave relief, the preconditions for which, as we have seen, were created already at the beginning of the century with the deepening of both the sculptural and emotional space of the figures.

The main feature of the development of the gravestone after the middle of the century is a tendency to excess. The size of the stele increases, as does the depth of the representation, the volumes of the figures and their expressive character. Grief is indicated through multifigural circular compositions, in which the shared pain seems to sweep away the living and the dead, relatives and friends. The faces, with their deepset eyes representing pain and their half-open mouths, have lost the grandeur characteristic of figures of the previous period. The very different general impression – restless, almost irritating – conveyed by this room in comparison with the corresponding room on the first floor, gives expression to the changed times. At the same time, the internalising of the pain of death isolates the figures, thus undermining any possibility of contact between the father, the wife and the son. The figures now stand parallel, gazing before them into space, each shut up in its own world and the pain of its eternal loneliness, almost ignoring the presence of the others.

These tendencies are reinforced by the simultaneous liberation of the individual from the moral shackles of the city-state, which reached the level of an overt demonstration of human vanity that was responsible for some of the most impressive of the contemporary Attic monuments. Many of these adorned the busy street along the Long Walls that linked Athens with the port of Piraeus.

The colossal seated lion from Moschato **no. 2677 (pl. 23)**, next to the staircase, comes from a monument of this kind, as do the large funeral monuments in the next room. The lion recalls (on a smaller scale) the series of earlier or contemporary monuments from Amphipolis and Chaironeia. The Moschato lion differs from these in that it appears, from the grave next to which it was found, to have been a private monument, and probably had reference to the courage of the deceased.

A similar spirit pervades the statue of the eagle **no. 4642.** The proud bird spreads its wings menacingly and turns its head with the deep-set Skopas-like eyes towards the snake, which has reared to strike at it – a vain endeavour, for its body is already in the eagle's claws. As early as Homer, the sighting of an eagle with a snake was an omen, a sign sent from the gods.

This group, therefore, probably crowned the grave monument of a seer. The style and free, realistic rendering of the wings foreshadow the art of the Hellenistic period.

By contrast, the highly interesting, roughly contemporary three-sided stele from Aigaleo at the centre of the room **(no. 2575)** should be attributed to a monument in honour of men who fell in war. This is made probable by the fact that the crowning is decorated with a helmet in the middle of each side, the crest of which forms a volute ornament.

Room 8 is specially designed at three levels to cater for the large (7 m. high) funerary monument from Kallithea. This marked the culmination of the monumental approach characteristic of tombstones

Impost block from a monument to the fallen, from Aigaleo.

of the third quarter of the 4th c. BC, and sets the tone for the room. The monument, to which we shall return directly, occupies virtually the whole of the lowest level at the back of the room, while the two higher levels are devoted to the contemporary development of the grave stele.

The first (top) level is dominated by the grave stele of Panchares, son of Leochares, **no. 5280,**[26] a work of unique size and decoration which adorned the grave of one of the Athenians killed at Chaironeia in 338 BC, as the lion of Moschato also probably did. The type of the tall, narrow stele crowned with a palmette and engraved with relief rosettes and the name of the dead person is an old one and continued to be found even after the prohibition of funerary monuments. Part of the way up, these stelai sometimes had a recess with a relief depiction of *dexiosis* or a funeral banquet. In the present stele, the heroic death of Panchares is depicted in this position. Only a single scene of the battle is rendered. Despite the 'heroic' nudity, the dead man is to be identified not with the warrior being trampled by the horse (this humiliating posture is inappropriate to the ancient view of heroic death), but with the standing hoplite facing the horseman who is attacking him from the right. It is clear from the coiffure and particularly the facial features, which strongly recall portraits of Alexander, that his foe was probably a Macedonian, and this reinforces the hypothesis that Panchares was indeed one of the thousand Athenian men who took part in this, the final great battle for Greek freedom. At the bottom of the stele is a loutrophoros with traces of a red band wrapped around it. The crowning member is missing, and there are no traces of where it was attached. An idea of its probable form is given by the contemporary rich palmette on display next to it.

The rest of the reliefs in the room transport us to another world. The relief from Pireos Street, **no. 5812** (next to the entrance), is a typical example of the full iconographic type of an Attic family

The grave stele of Panchares.

Grave stele no. 5812.

gravestone. The figures are arranged in a semicircle: opposite the woman seated on a throne, who died in childbirth, as is clear from the presence behind her of the maidservant holding the baby, stands her husband, with her mother in the background depicted frontally. The man and wife are virtually worked in the round. Both the stance and the drapery attest to the academic (Classicising) intent of the sculptor. The grieving

The grave stele of farewell.

expression of the mother is impressive; her facial features call to mind the work of Skopas and her stance figures on the sarcophagus with lamenting women from Sidon, which is attributed to the same sculptor. The attempt to render the baby with its little hat is also of interest.

The pathos typical of the grave monuments of this period is imprinted even more strongly on the emotionally charged family scene of the 'stele of farewell', next to it, **no. 429,** in which the figures are literally falling into each other's arms (the success enjoyed by this motif is demonstrated by the copy in the National Archaeological Museum), or in the fragmentary stele **no. 228** (next to the stele of Panchares), in which the depth of the pain is given independent sculptural form on the crowning through two lamenting women flanking the 'Muse from the Beyond', the Siren playing the kithara.

The development of the Classical plain grave stele with a palmette or pediment crowning and a relief loutrophoros – a category to which the large stele of Panchares belongs – can be followed in two more reliefs. One is the pedimental stele **no. 220,** which is halfway between the two family scenes mentioned above. In it, the handles of the loutrophoros are decorated with two youths in postures of dancing that recall works attributed to the contemporary sculptor Leochares.

In the pedimental stele **no. 2158** (in the middle of the wall, to the right of the entrance), which was the gravestone of the two brothers Sosimenes and Sokrates from the deme of Athmonon, there is a depiction on the loutrophoros of a *chous*, the gift usually presented to children at the Choai on the third day of the festival of the Anthesteria. The theory has been advanced that here the vases symbolise the ages of the deceased, of whom the former died unmarried (according to an earlier, now disputed theory, loutrophoroi were placed on the graves of people who died unwed), and the second while he was still a child. The very clear Dionysiac references (ivy around the neck) in the marble oinochoe **no. 3636,** with a scene of *dexiosis*, on display next to the staircase, recall the promise of eternity held out by the regenerated god Dionysos.

The third stele, **no. 428,** is crowned by a scene of butting rams (the painted palmette can just be seen below). This subject has reference to the daemonic force of nature, which is also expressed through the Archaic sphinxes or the lions on Classical tombs.

The monument of Kallithea.[27] The climax of the development of the grave stele and the funerary luxury of the second half of the 4th century BC is, of course, the monument of the Histrian metic Nikeratos son of Polyxenos and his son, Polyxenos son of Nikeratos. (The family is known epigraphically at Histria or Histros in Romania.) The monument was discovered in 1968 next to the Long Walls, near the Kallithea train station. The distant model for the monument was very probably the Mausoleum of Halikarnassos, which says much for the occupant's self-image. Fragments of a similar monument demonstrate that it was not unique in its day.

On a tall, slightly sloping pedestal crowned by a frieze with a scene of an Amazonomachy, with a crepis with three steps (the first with the names of the dead, the second with a frieze of monsters, lions and bulls at the corners) rises a funerary temple with two Ionic columns (**pl. 24**). Against the background of grey Eleusinian marble are projected three independent statues, facing the spectator. The central place is occupied by the son, who is flanked by his father on the right and a young slave on the left, carrying his master's himation.

The similarities with the group of Daochos at Delphi – the slender physique of the young athlete and the figure of the slave, who is covered by the folded himation – allow us to recognise the school of Lysippos, while the heavy figure of the father, with the himation tied around his waist, reveals some similarity with the later philosopher of Delphi. The monument is dated to some time after the Mausoleum, between the choregic monument of Lysikrates (335/4 BC) and the dedication of Daochos, that is at the beginning of the third quarter of the 4th century BC.

The surviving colours on the frieze (red cloaks and bronze-coloured breastplates and greaves of the Greeks, yellow short chitons of the Amazons) and on the temple (palmettes and astragals) indicate that the monument did not remain visible for long. Its destruction was probably due to some natural cause, such as an earthquake, or to the Ilissos stream, which at this point flowed through the Long Walls.

The same motif of the dead youth is reflected in a more traditional manner in the two stelai displayed in the area in front of the monument, on the middle level of the room. These are two versions of the figure of the young athlete, known from the stele from the Ilissos in the National Archaeological Museum. The pain of his premature loss is internalised very strongly by the youth, as can be seen from the superb head of the first, now fragmentary, stele **no. 5318,** an unpublished find from the north cemetery of the ancient Piraeus, in Thivon Street. The youth is accompanied by his young slave, as in the second stele **no. 2159** and the monument of Kallithea.

The loutrophoros of Lysis. Monuments like that of Kallithea provoked a reaction and prepared the ground for the legislation by which, two hundred years after Kleisthenes' law, Demetrios of Phaleron finally put an end to the art of the Attic grave relief. Much is said about this reaction to the provocation of monuments like that of Kallithea, especially on the part of the old Athenian families, by the modest loutrophoros with its commonplace depiction of a scene of *dexiosis* involving a man, which is displayed directly opposite to it at the top of the stairs.

It is genuinely moving suddenly to encounter, amongst the great number of anonymous grave monuments, the loutrophoros **no. 3280,** which adorned the tomb of Lysis, the pupil of Socrates known from the Platonic dialogue bearing his name, as is made clear by the name, patronymic and deme-name that can be read on the cylindrical base of the monument: Lysis, son of Demokrates, of the deme of Aixone. We learn from Plato that Lysis came from an old family of Aixoneus that claimed divine origins. The reason he chose to be buried in his property at Moschato is, of course, unknown: however, some role will undoubtedly have been played in the selection of this ordinary monument by the contempt felt by the old aristocrat for boastful nouveau riches like the Histrian metic.

Grave stele of a young athlete (330-320 BC).

ROOM 9

Sculptures of the Hellenistic period

This room, in which there are a few other works indicative of the style of the period, is devoted to the charming world of Hellenistic sculpture, which is dominated by female grace and childlike tenderness.

The small number of Hellenistic exhibits, in comparison with the large number and great wealth of the 4th-century output, is characteristic of the decline of Piraeus at this period. For virtually the whole of the 3rd century BC the city lived under Macedonian occupation, essentially cut off from Athens. This situation led to the decay of trade and the abandonment of the city and its harbours. A central position amongst the exhibits is occupied by the sculptures of the early Hellenistic period, the late 4th and early 3rd c. BC. In the middle is a statue of a young female deity or personification, **no. 5935,** dressed in a delicate, high-girt chiton and himation **(pl. 27),** a fine work of the late 4th c. BC recently acquired by the Museum (found in the rubbish dump at Ano Liosia).[28] A similar type is rendered by the female statue **no. 3637** displayed opposite, next to the door. The two statues are flanked by a group of votive statuettes of three young children in which can be recognised the Hellenistic sense of the tenderness of childhood. The statuette **no. 219** is earlier and more conservative in its form: it depicts a little girl raising the overfall of her peplos. Her neighbour, **no. 427,** is depicted leaning on a pillar with a goose in her hand and her legs crossed at the front (pl. 28). This reproduces a type commonly found in sanctuaries of the time.[29] This is also true of the naked boy with a ball **no. 246,** from the Asklepieion. The attribution of the other statuettes of young children to the Asklepieion or to the sanctuary of Artemis Munychia, on account of her relationship to Artemis Brauronia, is attractive, but cannot be proved The charming figure of a seated nymph **no. 1169,**[30] which for many years adorned the facade of a neoclassical house in Piraeus, is a Roman copy made in the 2nd c. AD of the famous group 'Invitation to a Dance', one of the most characteristic examples of the rococo current in Hellenistic sculpture. The Hellenistic art of the portrait is represented by the small head, crowned by a wreath, of a young ruler, dating from the 3rd c. BC, **no. 1765.** The epilogue to the long history of the grave relief, the flowering and decline of which we have followed in the previous rooms, was written by the ban on them imposed by Demetrios of Phaleron. The consequent disbanding of the sculpture workshops had long-term repercussions for the sculptural

type which is represented here only by the small relief of Demetrios and Hedyle **no. 2537,** dating from the end of the 3rd c. BC, which is in the Classical type of the *dexiosis*.

The nymph from the 'Invitation to a Dance' group (Roman copy).

ROOM 10

Art of the Roman period

This room contains representative examples of the basic spheres of output of neo-Attic art from the 1st to the 3rd c. AD: copies of Classical works, grave reliefs, and portraits.

In the imperial period, when Athens, under Roman protection, experienced a new flowering as the cultural capital of the empire, Piraeus enjoyed its share of imperial favour and the new prosperity, though the relinquishing of its leading position and the change in the commercial routes meant that it would never recover its old glory. A large part of the prosperity of Athens in the imperial period was due to tourism and the university life of the city. An important role, however, was played by the 'sculpture industry', which was based on the production of copies and variations of Classical works in a variety of sizes and types, such as the statues, reliefs and vases that decorated official or private Roman residences and gardens, the so-called Attic sarcophagi, and so on.

Neo-Attic decorative reliefs. The commercial character of this sphere of output is illustrated by the cargo of a trading ship that was wrecked, presumably by a clumsy manoeuvre, in the harbour of Piraeus, and was found by chance in 1933 during dredging work. The find consists of marble decorative reliefs which, as is clear from their uniformity of size, shape and borders, were intended to be incorporated into some luxurious building in Rome where, in fact, copies of them have been found – like the decoration on a closure slab from the wall of Nerva's forum.[31] The iconographic models are drawn from different periods and styles. They include motifs of the Severe Style, like the three Graces by the Boeotian sculptor Sokrates from the entrance to the Acropolis, Classical themes, such as the highly popular Amazonomachy that adorned the outside of the shield of Pheidias's Athena Parthenos, and

Late Classical subjects, such as the abduction of a woman (probably Iole) by Herakles **(pl. 29)** in a four-horse chariot led by a youth on foot ('leader of the bride') (a late 5th-century motif), Nymphs dancing, and Hermes bringing the infant Dionysos to the Nymph Nysa (4th c. BC). A separate, equally popular, category is formed by Archaising works, with the rigid, affected posture of the figures, standing on the tips of their toes, and the characteristic swallow-tails of the clothing. They are represented here by two types. The first has two depictions set side by side: the contest for the Delphic tripod between Apollo and Herakles and, next to and completely unconnected with it, a scene of sacrifice **(pl. 30)**. The second has a procession of gods (Athens, Apollo and Artemis) led by Hermes. The copies were enlivened by many variations, as, for example, in the coiffure and garments of the Graces or the background of the Amazonomachy scene **(pl. 31),** and interventions were also made that altered the style of the composition, such as the altar with the tree and the additional woman in the dance of the Nymphs. From the same find comes the Classicising Sphinx wearing a polos adorned by a palmette. A feature of all these works is the coldness of the technically flawless Hadrianic copies, though they also exhibit a number of later elements (e.g. the use of the drill) that date the find to the middle of the 2nd c. AD.

Copies of sculptures. A sample of the choices and the manner of working of the copies is provided by two unfinished figures: that of the Athena from the west pediment of the Parthenon **(no. 252)** and a Hellenistic Artemis Agrotera (goddess of hunting) **(no. 39).** The external appearance and social position of the artists is described by Lucian in his autobiographical *Dreams '[Sculpture] was a working-class hermaphrodite with unkempt hair, her hands full of calluses, and her robe tied around the waist with a belt, and she was covered with dust, like my uncle when he's at work. Elsewhere, he says ... and even if you become a Pheidias or a Polykleitos and make many admirable works, everyone will* *praise your art, but none of those that see you, if they have any sense, will want to be like you, because you will be like a working man who lives from the labour of his hands.* The middle of the room is occupied by the larger than life size statue of a youth **no. 4498 (pl. 32),** a copy dating from the Antonine period of a Hermes of post-Polykleitian type that was found in Kephisia, a popular suburb of Roman Athens.[32] Next to it is a statuette of a Maenad with an inset head **(no. 212),** a fine copy dating from the 2nd c. AD.

Grave stelai from the 1st c. BC to the 3rd c. AD. Opposite are four representative examples of the development of the grave relief, dating from the 1st c. BC and the 1st, 2nd and 3rd c. AD. The series begins at the right with stele **no. 388,** of the 1st c. BC, depicting a child resting its right arm on a hermaic stele, with his dog to his left. The body and the border (consisting of Corinthian columns and antefixes) is Hellenistic in conception. The frontal approach to the figure is shared by the following pieces. In the other reliefs is to be found the now fully developed type of the Roman grave monument, with the dead person rendered frontally and enclosed within an arched border, the outer corners of which are adorned by rosettes. All the reliefs have connecting dowels in the sides. In the first, dating from the 1st c. AD **(no. 223),** the youth is a rigid figure, resting his arm on a Siren playing the kithara; the base is decorated by two Tritons. The depiction of the female figure in the type of the Herculaneum Woman is more conventional in the next relief, **no. 215,** of the 2nd. c. AD. The grave stele **no. 1160** is of great interest, because of the spread of the cult of Isis to virtually the entire eastern Mediterranean. (There was a temple to her in Piraeus as early as the 4th c. BC.) The stele is that of Ammia Bibullia daughter of Philokrates of Sounion, who was a priestess of the Egyptian goddess, as is clear from her coiffure, the way the chiton is tied in the middle of the breast, and the cult vessels – the sistrum and the bucket containing Nile water.

Portraits. At the back of the room is displayed a selection of portraits of emperors, Roman officials, and members of the local aristocracy, covering the same period, from the 1st to the 3rd c. AD. The earliest of them is the portrait of Claudius **no. 1163** (AD 41-45); next to it is the inset head of a larger than life size statue of Trajan, **no. 276** (AD 98-117). Between them are the busts of a general wearing a breastplate, contemporary with Trajan **(no. 1162),** and a 2nd c. AD Athenian, Gaius Memmius Threptos from the deme of Lamptrai, who himself dedicated the bust to Zeus Hypsistos **(no. 272).** The last in the series is the realistic portrait of an unknown subject, which has the harsh features and short beard characteristic of faces in the hard 3rd c. AD **(no. 275).** In the middle and at the right are two majestic colossal statues of the philhellene emperor Hadrian, who was a great benefactor of Athens and Piraeus (AD 117-138). These statues are of a size unique in Greece (over 3 m. high). The emperor is depicted wearing a breastplate and paludamentum, with his left leg resting on an elevation. The statues were found in neighbouring plots of land in the harbour, and were probably intended for export. The inset head of the first **(no. 1197-1199),** with wreath **(no. 33),** is preserved. The second is headless and is identified thanks to the known decoration of the emperor's breastplate (palladion resting on the Roman she-wolf, being crowned by two Victories). In the back of the room, at the right, is the headless statue of an unknown subject, wearing the toga, the characteristic dress of the Roman citizen, 2nd. c. AD **(no. 277).** At the left is the rare portrait of one of the least-known emperors, the patrician Balbinus, who reigned for three months in AD 238 **(no. 278).** In the Museum storeroom is to be found an identical base (with the eagle and only the legs), which probably belonged to a second statue of Balbinus or his co-emperor Pupianus.

*Colossal head of the emperor
Trajan (AD 98-117).*

*Portrait of the emperor Claudius
(AD 41-54).*

Statue of the emperor Balbinus (AD 238).

NOTES - BIBLIOGRAPHY

The bibliography is restricted to special studies dealing with exchibits in the Museum, with emphasis on more recent finds. The only exception is the history of Attic grave reliefs.

1. Lionel Casson - J. Richard Steffy edd., *The Athlit Ram*, Texas University Press, 1991.

2. Ch. Saatsoglou - Paliadeli, "Μαρμάρινοι Οφθαλμοί από το λιμάνι του Πειραιά", *Αρχαιολογική Εφημερίς*, 1978, pp. 15- 34.

3. H. Frost, "Pyramidal" Stone Anchors: an Inquiry, *Proceedings of the 1st International Symposium on Ship Construction in Antiquity*, Tropis I (H. Tzalas ed.), Piraeus, 1985, pp. 97 - 114.

4. I. Dekoulakou - Sideris, "A Metrological Relief from Salamis", *American Journal of Archaeology*, 94, 1990, pp. 445 - 451.

5. G. Steinhauer, "Inscription Agoranomique du Pirée", *Bulletin de Correspondance Hellénique*, 118, 1994, pp. 51 - 68.

6. E. Mastrokostas, "Αλάβαστρα του 700 π.Χ. εκ της ανασκαφής του βωμού του Διός επί της κορυφής της Πάρνηθος", *Annuario* 45, 1983, pp. 339 - 344.

7. L. Palaiokrassa, *Το ιερό της Αρτέμιδος Μουνιχίας*, Athens, 1991.

8. I. Sakellarakis, "Το μινωικό ιερό κορυφής των Κυθήρων", *ΛΟΙΒΗ εις μνήμην Ανδρέα Γ. Καλοκαιρινού*, Heraklion, 1994, pp.195- 203, id. "Μινωικό χάλκινο ειδώλιο σκορπιού από τα Κύθηρα", *Έπαινος Ιωάννου Κ. Παπαδημητρίου* (ed. B. Χ. Πετράκος), Athens, 1997, pp. 243 - 272.

9. *Αρχαιολογική Εφημερίς*, 1916, p. 8, 1948 - 1949, p. 114, *American Journal of Archaeology*, 54, 1950, pp. 1-9, Αρχαιολογικόν Δελτίον, 17, 1961- 1962, p. 39, Αρχαιολογικόν Δελτίον, 20, 1965, pp. 125, *Αρχαιολογικόν Δελτίον*, 23, 1968, p. 113, H. Tzavella- Evjen, "A Mycenan Tomb at Salamis", *Αρχαιολογική Εφημερίς*, 131, 1992, pp. 67 - 93.

10. I. Polychronakou - Sgouritsa, "Το μυκηναϊκό νεκροταφείο της Βάρκιζας/ Βάρης", *Αρχαιολογικόν Δελτίον* 43, 1988, Μέρος Α, Μελέτες, Athens, 1995, pp. 1 - 108.

11. D. I. Skilardi, "Ανασκαφή παρά τα Μακρά Τείχη και η οινοχόη του Ταύρου", *Αρχαιολογική Εφημερίς*, 1975 (1976), pp. 66 -149.

12. H. Metzger, "Lebès fragmentaire de la collection Géroulanos", *Studies in*

honor of T.B.L. Webster, II, pp. 83 - 88.

13. F. Eckstein, "Τα χάλκινα του Πειραιά", *Επετηρίς ΦΣΠΘ,* 15, 1976, pp. 35- 50, M. Donderer, Oesterr. Jahreshefte 61, 1991-92, C. Houser, *Greek Monumental Bronze Sculpture of the Fifth and Fourth Centuries B.C.,* 1987.

14. G. Richter, Kouroi[3] No. 159 bis, N. Kontoleon, "Zur archaischen Bonzestatue aus dem Piraeus", *Opus Nobile,* Festschrift U. Jantzen (1969), p. 91 ff., id., *Aspects de la Grèce Préclassique,* pp. 81 f.f. και p. 92, K. Wallenstein, *Korinthische Plastik des 7. und 6. Jahrhunderts vor Christus* (1971) p. 163 f.f., G. Dontas, *Archaische und klassische griechische Plastik, Akten des internationalen Kolloquiums vom 22. - 25. April 1985 in Athen,* 1986, I, pp. 181 - 192, W. Fuchs, *Die Skulptur der Griechen, München*[4], 1993, p. 42.

15. D. Ohly, *Archäologischer Anzeiger* 1971, pp. 580, M. Ohly - Dumm and M. Robertson, *Αρχαιολογικά Ανάλεκτα εξ Αθηνών,* XIV, 1981, pp. 127 f.f.

16. Αρχαιολογικά Ανάλεκτα εξ Αθηνών, I, 34 κ.ε., *Bulletin de Correspondance Hellénique,* XCII, 754.

17. G. Dontas, "La grande Artémis du Pirée: une oeuvre d' Euphranor", *Antike Kunst* 25, 1987, pp. 15 - 34.

18. K. Schefold, "Die Athene des Piraeus", *Antike Kunst* 14, 1971, p. 37 f.f., G.B. Waywell, "Athena Mattei", *Annual of the British School at Athens,* 66, 1971, p. 373 f.f., O. Palagia, *Αρχαιολογικά Ανάλεκτα εξ Αθηνών,* VI, 1973, pp. 323 - 329, ιδ., Euphranor, 1980, A. Stewart, Greek Scuplture, London, 1990, p. 179.

19. I. Ch. Papachristodoulou, "Άγαλμα και ναός Κυβέλης εν Μοσχάτω Αττικής", *Αρχαιολογική Εφημερίς,* 1973, p. 213 f.f.

20. I. Petrocheilos, "Αναθηματικά γλυπτά της Κυβέλης από τον Πειραιά", *Αρχαιολογική Εφημερίς,* 1992, pp. 21 - 65.

21. J. M. Dentzer, "Un nouveau relief du Pirée et le type du banquet attique au V s. av. J.C.", *Bulletin de Correspondance Hellénique,* XCIV, pp. 67 - 90.

22. I. Jucker, "Artemis Kindyas", *Gestalt und Geschichte, Festschrift Karl Schefold* (=*Antike Kunst* Beiheft 4, 1967), pp. 133 f.f.

23. E. Conze, *Die attischen Grabreliefs,* Berlin 1893-1922, H. Diepolder, *Die attischen Grabreliefs des 5. und 4. Jahrhundrts v. Chr.,* Berlin, 1931 (fundamental for the evolution of the form of Attic grave stellai in 5th and 4th c. BC.), B. Schmaltz, *Griechische Grabreliefs,* Darmstadt, 1983 (general introduction to the

subject, with bibliography), C.W. Clairmont, *Classical Attic Tombstones,* 1993 (catalogue of Classical Attic Funerary monuments), J. Bergemann, *Demos und Thanatos,* München, 1997. Λουτροφόροι: G. Kokula, Marmorlutrophoren, Köln, 1974, Λήκυθοι: B. Schmaltz, *Untersuchungen zu den attischen Marmorlekythen,* Berlin 1970.

24. I. Tsirivakos, "Ηνίοχος Τέχνης Τραγικής", *Αρχαιολογικόν Δελτίον,* 29, 1974, Μέρος Α, Μελέται, Athens, 1977, pp. 88ι- 94.

25. A. Kaloyeropoulou, "Τέσσερα επιτύμβια κλασσικά ανάγλυφα από την Αττική", *Έπαινος Ιωάννου Κ. Παπαδημητρίου* (ed. Β. Χ. Πετράκος), Athens, 1997, pp. 231 - 252.

26. E. Papastavrou, "Η επιτύμβια στήλη 5280 του Μουσείου Πειραιά", *Αρχαιολογική Εφημερίς,* 127, 1988, pp. 61 - 70.

27. E. Tsirivakos, "Kallithea: Ergebnisse der Ausgrabung", *Αρχαιολογικά Ανάλεκτα εξ Αθηνών,* IV, 1971, pp. 108 - 110.

28. Chr. Vorster, Griechische Kinderstatuen (doctoral diss.), Köln, 1983, pp. 349.

29. M. I. Pologiorgi, "Το γυναικείο άγαλμα του Αρχαιολογικού Μουσείου Πειραιώς αρ. ευρ. 5935", *Regional Schools in Hellenistic Sculpture, Proceedings of an International Conference held at the American School of classical Studies at Athens,* March 15 - 17, 1996, O. Palagia and W. Coulson edd., Oxbow Monograph 19, 1998, pp. 35 - 46

30. Y. Despinis, "Σημειώσεις από το Μουσείο του Πειραιά (I)" *Αρχαιολογικόν Δελτίον,* 20, 1965, Αθήνα, 1966, pp. 133 - 134.

31. Th. Stephanidou - Tiveriou, Νεοαττικά. *Οι ανάγλυφοι πίνακες από το λιμάνι του Πειραιά,* Athens, 1979.

32. D. Kazianis, "Άγαλμα της Ρωμαιοκρατίας από την Κηφισιά", *Αρχαιολογικά Ανάλεκτα εξ Αθηνών,* XV, 1982, pp. 130 - 141.

33. J. M. Toynbee, "Four Roman Portraits in the Piraeus Museum", *Annual of the British School at Athens,* 53 - 54, 1958- 1959, pp. 285 - 291.

34. P. Zoridis, Δύο πορτραίτα του Αδριανού του τύπου "Rollockenfrisur" από τον Πειραιά και την Επίδαυρο", *Αρχαιολογικά Ανάλεκτα εξ Αθηνών,* XV, 1982 pp. 115 - 124.

PLATES

1. Bronze ram from a trireme.

2. Metrological relief.

3. Mycenaean krater with a depiction of a chariot.

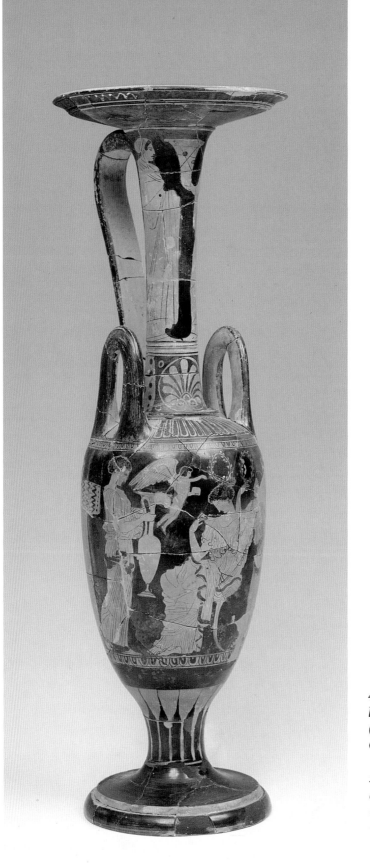

4. Red-figure loutrophoros (Yeroulanos Collection).

5. Red-figure amphora (Yeroulanos Collection).

6. Doll (plangon) of Classical date.

7. Figurine of a squatting woman. Hellenistic perio

8. Corinthian helmet. 7th c. BC.

9. Chalkidian helmet. 6th c. BC.

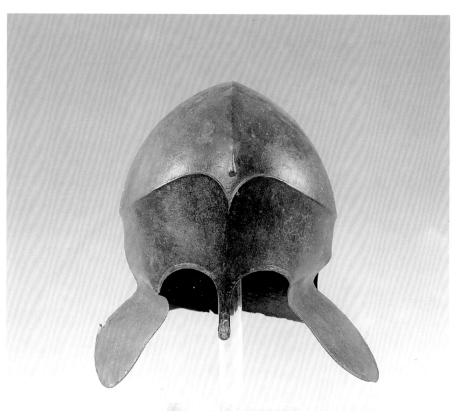

10. Red-figure lekythos with a depiction
of a wood-cutter.

11. Melian relief with a depiction of Herakles
and Nessos.

*12. Archaic
bronze Apollo
(height 1.95 m.)*

14. Bronze tragic mask

13. Bronze statue of Artemis (height 1.94 m.).

16. Votive relief from the Asklepieion in Piraeus.

15. Bronze statue of Artemis (height 1.55 m.).

18. *Grave stele of an actor from Salamis.*

17. *Grave stele of Chairedemos and Lykeas.*

19. Grave stele of Hippomachos and Kallias.

20. Grave stele of a woman from Glyphada, Attica.

21. *Grave stele of Aget...*
of Megara.

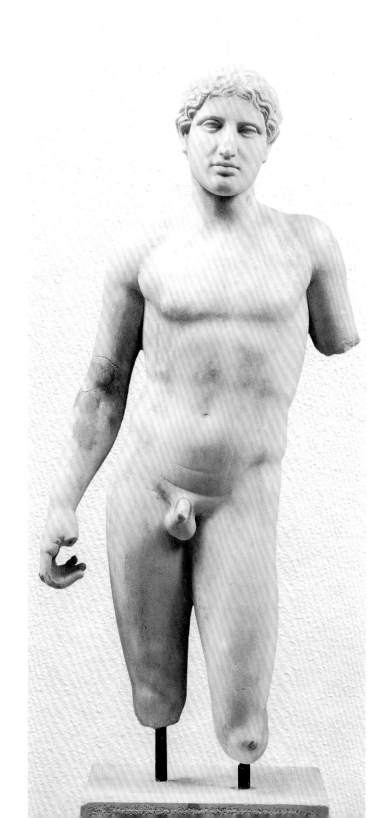

*22. Funerary statuette
of a young athlete.*

23. The funerary lion
from Moschato.

24. The monument
of Kallithea:
the temple.

25, 26. The monument of Kallithea: details from the frieze on the base.

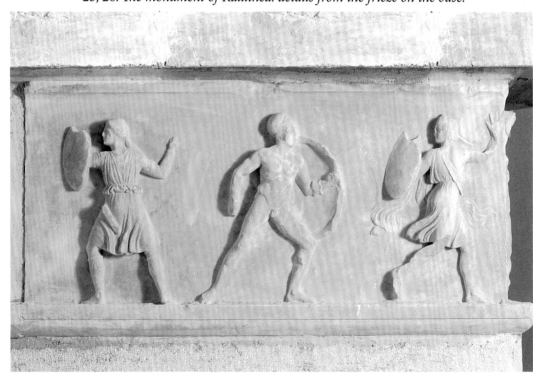

27. Female torso. Hellenistic period.

28. Neo-Attic decorative relief with a depiction of an abduction.

29. Hellenistic statuette of a little girl, from a sanctuary in Piraeus.

30. *Neo-Attic decorative slab with Archaic scenes.*

31. *Neo-Attic decorative slab with a copy of the Amazonomachy scene on the shield of Athena Parthenos.*

32. *The youth of Kephisia.*
Roman copy of a 4th c. BC
original.

33. Colossal portrait of the emperor Hadrian.

Editor: GEORGE STEINHAUER
Translation: DAVID HARDY
Art editors: MANOLIA SKOULOUDI, YANNIS YARMENITIS

Production - Printing: M. TOUBIS S.A.